The
R Yellow Brick
Road

A WOMAN'S JOURNEY TO THE EDGE AND BACK

Be Encouraged!

Gail

Gail A. Sullivan

The Yellow Brick Road

A WOMAN'S JOURNEY TO THE EDGE AND BACK

By Gail A. Sullivan

Unless otherwise noted, Scriptures are taken from the Holy Bible, New International Version. Copyright 1973, 1978, 1984 by International Bible Society.

Cover design: Brave Nu Digital, www.bravenudigital.com
Interior design: Toolbox Creative, www.toolboxcreative.com

Library of Congress Cataloguing-in-Publications Data
Library of Congress Control Number: 2010909448
Author Gail A. Sullivan
The Yellow Brick Road
ISBN: 978-1-4507-2099-1
Library of Congress subject headings:
1. Self-help Christian 2. Philosophy, Psychology, Religion

2010

Dedication

This book is dedicated to every woman who finds herself on a journey, who's not quite sure where the road is going, but knows, deep down inside, that she must follow it. May you find hope in knowing that you are not the first to go down such a dangerous path. Others have made it. I have made it. And you will make it too! Know that you never have to travel through life alone… God is only a prayer away!

IN MEMORY OF

In memory of my dad,

~ **Thomas Murray Murphy** ~

I never grew tired of sitting at his feet and listening to

his life's journey through stories.

He was an amazing man!

I love him and I miss him.

ACKNOWLEDGEMENTS

There are so many people to thank and I don't want to miss one of them, for success is never accomplished alone, but through the actions of many.

I start with my children, whom I love dearly. I'm sorry that when the journey got rough, I wasn't fully there, but I'm so glad that the God I always told you about watched over us, and brought us through. Thank you for hanging in there with me. You are the most amazing people I know and it's a privilege to travel with you on this journey called life.

I'm thankful for the love of my Mother, Father, and sister, Margaret, who being older and wiser, demonstrated their unconditional love toward me in the darkest of times and never judged me.

The prayers of my church family and friends were abundant, I'm sure. Thank you for taking those moments in prayer to lift up my family and I when prompted by the Spirit. Know that those little prayers resulted in explosions of miracles in our lives!

I never could have made it through Oz without my friends: Steve, Lynn and Matt. I'm not sure you'll ever really know the impact you had on my survival. I guess friends never realize that because they are just busy being friends. Your gracious investment in my life will never be forgotten. Thank you.

Thanks to Brenda who was like a surrogate big sister to me when I needed that most. Know that your friendship was a blessing!

To all the professional organizations and individuals who reached out and touched my life, doing what they do everyday, thank you! It's easy to wonder if you make a difference in your profession. You made a difference to me! You provided me with services and words of encouragement that kept me moving forward, day in and day out, on this incredible and difficult journey. I couldn't have done it without you all!

A major THANK YOU goes to Melissa Miller, my Wizard of Oz, whose counsel and friendship brought me home to wholeness. It's a difficult task to unload your thoughts and feelings, along with your life story to a stranger. You became my confidant in the darkest of places. In that office I found an abundance of God's love, wisdom, patience, and kindness that ultimately led to a miraculous healing. He used you powerfully! Thank you. Thank you. Thank you.

There are many people in this book whose names are not specifically mentioned but who were all part of the cast of characters in my story. Regardless of how big or small your part was, your encouraging words and actions were critical to my healing. Never underestimate the power of a kind deed or word given in love.

Although my journey through Oz came to an end, the work was not finished by far, and neither are my words of thanks.

There are four individuals who were critical to this book being finished.

Thank you, Matt, for your consistent encouragement to write, write, write.

Thank you, Jan, for coaching me through the publishing process.

Thank you, Christin, for your expertise in writing and editing, and the many hours you gave me.

Thank you, Gabe, for your cunning creative eye and marketing skills.

A big THANK YOU also goes to the many girlfriends I have at BECAUSE WOMEN. Your excitement and enthusiasm at seeing this book published fueled me in the final publishing days! I may be out of Oz, but I am in an amazing place with incredible women who have their own stories to share! Your energy and words of praise have strengthened and encouraged me beyond measure!

It wouldn't be right to end this list of thanks without mentioning those who have invested into my life spiritually as mentors. Thank you, Rev. Pasco and Mary Ann Manzo. Your discipleship and close friendship over the last 27 years has profoundly molded me into the Woman of Faith I am today.

Thank you to Pastor Larry Baucom and the ministerial staff of Suncoast Community Church. The ministry of love that you extended to me was essential to my not being spiritually homeless in such a difficult and confusing time. I truly appreciate you and your ministry.

Thank you also Pastor Vincent Smith, III and First Lady Venetta Smith for welcoming me into your church at a most critical time in my life. Your love, your preaching, your prayers and your praise to God, as well as the kindness of your congregation have brought spiritual healing and restoration to my soul.

Thanks be to God, the author and finisher of my Faith, my constant companion, and closest of friends. To Him be the glory!

TABLE OF CONTENTS

"You must walk. It is a long journey, through a country that is sometimes pleasant and sometimes dark and terrible."

L. Frank Baum

The Wonderful Wizard of Oz

Chapter 1 | THE STORM

Like a cyclone raging across the Kansas prairie, it tore
through my life, ripping up everything and everyone in its
path. It was dark and scary, confusing and unexpected. Inside
my own home, I was tossed and tumbled about, not knowing
whether I was right side up or upside down. The name of
this great storm was "Divorce." It had already destroyed
others, and now it had ravaged its way into my life. And
like Dorothy from Kansas, I was totally unprepared for the
incredible journey that lay ahead.

Whether you call it a twister, a cyclone, or a tornado, it
is one of Mother Nature's most devastating storms. It starts
with the convergence of two different air masses. When
the conditions are just right, a vortex forms — and before
you know it, the spinning storm is well on its way, leaving
destruction in its wake.

Divorce is one of life's greatest and most destructive storms. There are many different components and scenarios that can set it off. Once it's in full force, marriages and families are often wiped out by its brutal effects. Lives are changed forever.

In *The Wonderful Wizard of Oz* by L. Frank Baum, we meet the young, pleasant, and somewhat naïve Dorothy. We're told that Dorothy was adopted by her Uncle Henry and Aunt Em, so we don't know if she's ever experienced a Kansas twister before. This type of storm was not an unusual occurrence for Uncle Henry and Aunt Em, however. Kansas is smack in the middle of what many people refer to today as "Tornado Alley." Annually, the United States averages about 1,000 of these violent storms, and it is here, in Tornado Alley, that they emerge most often.

As for me, I grew up in the age of "Divorce Alley." Statistically speaking, divorce had been on the rise for as long as I could remember. With every decade, it seemed to become more common and widely accepted by society as a whole. I don't think anybody getting married ever really expects to one day be divorced. Most people walking down the aisle assume that they will be married forever. I had married a Christian man—a minister at that. I never for a moment even considered the possibility that I would ever be caught in the path of a destructive storm like this. I had no emergency plan in place.

Dorothy's Uncle Henry, on the other hand, was the perfect storm captain of his day. He understood the importance of always being alert. While Dorothy went about her everyday routine, it was Uncle Henry who noticed the sudden darkening of the sky. He sensed the change in the air. He observed the grass bowing in the wind, rippling like waves. And he heard the roar of the cyclone bearing down on his farm.

"Head for the storm cellar!" he shouted.

But Dorothy didn't make it on time, and neither did I.

I NEVER FOR A MOMENT EVEN CONSIDERED THE POSSIBILITY THAT I WOULD EVER BE CAUGHT IN THE PATH OF A DESTRUCTIVE STORM LIKE THIS. I HAD NO EMERGENCY PLAN IN PLACE.

Dorothy clasped her dog, Toto, close to her heart and held on for dear life as her house was lifted into the air, spinning uncontrollably in the whirlwinds of the storm. In the movie version, Dorothy watches helplessly as all of her family and friends, barn animals, and yard debris go flying past her window. Even Mrs. Gulch is caught up in the treacherous winds, peddling her bicycle to that infamous musical jingle as she's transformed into a wicked witch on a broomstick. No one is safe. Nothing is secure.

I felt the same way. As the judge's gavel fell and he pronounced the end of my nineteen and a half year marriage, I, too, was caught up into the vortex of a storm. I was bewildered by how quickly this powerful storm took control. I held on to my children while everything around me began spinning. My marriage was gone in minutes. In addition, I watched helplessly, as my lifelong dreams flew by me, disassembling themselves right in front of my eyes. There went my identity, right out the window, and my self-image, right behind it. My confidence was shattered and my heart was broken beyond repair. Everything I knew—all that I built, all that I owned, all that I collected—was uprooted and displaced. I tried to pick up the pieces, but they slipped through my fingers. I felt numb. I couldn't focus. My spirit was crushed. For the first time in my life, I was sad… very, very sad, and close to hopelessness.

Chapter 2 | SOMEWHERE OVER THE RAINBOW

Dorothy screamed as her bed slid back and forth across the room, while the house spiraled downward, plummeting to the earth. She gasped as it hit the ground with a thud. Picking up her basket in one hand, and Toto in the other, she immediately headed for the front door. In the blink of an eye, everything was transformed from black and white to brilliant Technicolor. I remember how amazing it was, as a child watching the movie, to see Dorothy set out from her broken down farmhouse into this wonderful new land. Dorothy's eyes opened wide as she took in the colorful hues of the gigantic flowers that surrounded her. The sight was magnificent! The air was peaceful and the birds chirped softly and melodically. Scanning her new surroundings, breathing it all in, she exclaimed, "Toto, I have a feeling we're not in Kansas anymore."

Miraculously, Dorothy emerged from the rubble, totally unscathed—every hair in place, her ringlets gently falling over her shoulders. The camera moved in for a close up and we could see her lipstick was perfect, as she said with a smile, "We must be over the rainbow!"

I'm afraid I wasn't so optimistic and enthusiastic about my new surroundings. For one thing, a lot of it looked the same. I still lived in the same house, slept in the same bed, and worked at the same job—but everything seemed off-kilter and out of focus. I couldn't quite put my finger on it, but something had changed. Could it have been me? Dazed and confused, I puttered around, trying to go about my everyday life, but as depression set in, my world darkened.

One morning, shortly after the finalization of the divorce, I woke up with a weird feeling that something very unusual had occurred overnight. My face felt as if my skin had shifted into a different position. It was very strange! Muscles I had never used before were pushing themselves into an awkward and uncomfortable position. I rushed to the bathroom mirror and was shocked at what I saw. My beautiful smile had turned itself upside down. A frown was permanently fixed on my face. As I leaned in closer to the mirror, I pushed the sides of my lips upward into their proper place. Over and over, without fail, they fell back to their new designated setting. This was not good! My face was now reflecting the sadness of my soul. I was disheartened and afraid as the tears streamed down my cheeks.

In anger and disbelief, I shouted, "A frown? A frown?"

FOR ME, IT WAS THE FIRST MAJOR SIGN THAT I HAD GONE FROM A WORLD OF JOYFUL COLOR TO A WORLD OF BLACK AND WHITE.

For me, it was the first major sign that I had gone from a world of joyful color to a world of black and white. It would be a long time before a smile would visit my face again. I'd catch a glimpse of it now and then, on occasion, but it never stayed for very long.

You may think it strange, that such a simple thing had such a powerful effect on me. Sure, like everyone, I had experienced both good days and bad in my life. But I had never really frowned before. I always attempted to make the best of each day, and I found that putting on a smile would always start me off on the right track. A smile could lead to "Good Mornings!" and "Hellos!" along with compliments, words of encouragement, handshakes, and even hugs. It could make the dreariest day seem brighter.

Now I would have to paint a smile on each day. It would no longer be genuinely fueled by the joy of my heart. It would be an attempt to mask what was really going on inside. It took a lot of effort, but I forced myself to do it.

Dorothy sings of a place "where troubles melt like lemon drops," but my troubles were more like bitters that continually multiplied. My head was so foggy, it was hard to carry on any detailed conversation. And for a woman with the gift of gab, I suddenly didn't have much to say.

I have always believed that a conversation filled with negativity is dangerous and potentially damaging to those who hear it. My heart was filled with anger, pain, and discouragement. I felt that if I talked about it out loud, I would be giving way to an avalanche of destructive defeatism. Enough damage had already been done. I didn't want to be responsible for creating any more. I decided it would be best to say nothing at all.

I did, however, pray—a lot! I asked God to help me to hold it all together. I asked him to help me to face this new world every day. I asked Him to help me get out of the house, make it to work, and return back again, without completely falling apart. And He did.

Chapter 3 | DORTHY AND TOTO, TOO

Although Dorothy was not prepared for the adventure that awaited her, she found comfort knowing that she was not alone. Her closest friend and most faithful companion was her dog, Toto. Other than the clothes on her back and the basket in her hand, Toto was all that remained from her old life in Kansas. She had held on tightly to him as they fell from the sky, and in return, he would stay by her side throughout her journey.

I, on the other hand, felt isolated and very much alone in this new place. I looked around for encouragement, but it wasn't there. Truthfully, my family and friends wanted to be supportive, but I put up walls between us. I told myself I didn't want to worry them. If I kept a smile on my face and held them at arms' length, maybe I could hide my immense brokenness.

It was a huge decision to get divorced, one I have never regretted. But now I had to take responsibility to walk in that decision. There were many phone calls, and multitudes of prayers, that I was extremely grateful for, but in the end I had a journey ahead of me. It wouldn't be long before God would bring people into my life to help me. They would be local people, whose part in my life, whether great or small, would be critical to my ultimate healing.

Right now, I was embarrassed that my marriage was over. I had failed! What would people say? Had I not tried hard enough to make it work? Was my faith not strong enough? Were my prayers not long enough? Would people think that my God wasn't big enough? Maybe if I just didn't talk about it, neither would anyone else. My hope was that eventually we would all see how God would work all things out for the good. I had spent so much of my life witnessing for this wonderful God, I cringed as I thought how all those great stories would be tossed away by onlookers, thinking it was just another religious gimmick that failed. I didn't want to see God discounted or discredited that way.

I HAD SPENT SO MUCH OF MY LIFE WITNESSING FOR THIS WONDERFUL GOD, I CRINGED AS I THOUGHT HOW ALL THOSE GREAT STORIES WOULD BE TOSSED AWAY BY ONLOOKERS, THINKING IT WAS JUST ANOTHER RELIGIOUS GIMMICK THAT FAILED. I DIDN'T WANT TO SEE GOD DISCOUNTED OR DISCREDITED THAT WAY.

Although outwardly, I remained composed and appeared to hold it all together, inwardly, my heart, mind and emotions were crumbling fast. I had to face the reality of how much I had lost, literally overnight. I'm not talking about money or property. We didn't have much to divide, so we were able to settle things quickly, fairly, and amicably. It was the loss of the marriage, and the life's dream that came with it—as well as the partnership in ministry I believed I was destined for—that was so difficult to accept.

After almost twenty years, my marriage to David had officially come to an end, and the grief was unbearable. How could this have happened to me? I had been so committed. I had tried so hard to do all the right things. I had prayed so faithfully and consistently, over the years, for my husband and for our marriage. So how could all those good and right actions end up in such a mess?

With the end of the marriage came the dissolution of a life's dream together—all the things we had hoped for and worked toward as a couple. There were things we wanted to accomplish, places we wanted to travel to. Nearest and dearest to my heart were the lives that I believed we would touch through our partnership in ministry, a partnership I thought had always worked so well.

Eventually I would discover that a new dream awaited me, and many of the things that were so important to me were not lost forever, but would reappear later. I just couldn't picture it at this time. Everything seemed lost. Yet I knew I still had the two things that were most precious to me: my faith and my children.

I must admit, I didn't get it at first. I thought I had arrived in Oz alone. I was so displaced and disheveled emotionally that it didn't dawn on me until much later that my three teenage children had come along for the ride and experienced some significant emotional blows themselves from the impact of this storm. That grieved me.

I had always been very actively involved in my children's lives. Long before the birth of our first child, I had decided I would be a stay-at-home mom. By the time my daughter Jordan was ready for kindergarten, I knew I wanted to homeschool her and her siblings, Joe and Grace. We always did everything together. Even though we never had a lot of money, we had a good time. We would sing together, pray together, and play together, learning as we went through each day. One year when we didn't have a television, I read aloud for hours each night, on my bed, with the children snuggled around me, begging for one more chapter before the lights went out. I loved being a mom, and I loved being in the middle of all three of my kids' lives, supporting them in everything they did.

My husband pastored a church for eight and a half years. As the pastor's wife, it was my job, among other things, to run the children's ministry. I was constantly putting together story hours, Sunday school lessons, vacation Bible activities, along with other events for all the children in the church, as well as the community. This allowed me the liberty of being involved with the things my children were interested in.

When our time at the church came to an end, God opened a door for me to teach at a private Christian school. I had really enjoyed concentrating on being a pastor's wife and immersing myself in all that the full-time ministry brought with it. But I discovered that teaching school could be just as much of a blessing. Those wonderful third graders loved me and I loved them back. My children were also able to attend the school. We would ride off to school each morning and return home at night in the car together. After homeschooling, private school was a good experience for them.

Within two years, my husband decided to leave the ministry and go to work full time as a police officer. As much as I liked working at the school and being in such close proximity to my children, I sensed God leading me to rejoin the corporate world. I really struggled with the decision, but God convinced me that my children would never learn to listen to His voice, if my voice was always so close and so constant in their lives. He assured me they would take care of one another. So I enrolled the kids in public school and eventually went to work in a large investment firm. Years later, as I went through my divorce, I realized that this business career was God's way of providing for me and the children financially through the difficult times that lay ahead.

The children had begun experiencing my "checking out" emotionally about four years prior to the divorce. That's how long it was from when I found out about the multiple encounters of infidelity, to the actual divorce, itself. Four years were invested in trying to save the marriage. Although the children saw my constant sadness from day one, they never understood what it was all about. I always kept hidden the marital difficulties that we were going through. Five months before the divorce, my husband and I separated. It wasn't until I actually filed for divorce, three months later, that I sat down with each of the children, and explained in detail, why.

Honestly, I didn't know how to handle the situation, at the time. Even now, I'm not sure that there is a right or wrong way. But I do know this: there are times in our lives when we have to take a close look at everything, pray, and make the decision to do what we believe is best for everyone involved. During that time, I seriously believed that my husband and I would somehow pull it all together, and our marriage would be restored. I couldn't justify telling the children a lot of adult information that I knew would hurt them and possibly turn them away from their father, if there was no reason to. Right or wrong, that's how it went down.

ALTHOUGH THE CHILDREN SAW MY CONSTANT SADNESS FROM DAY ONE, THEY NEVER UNDERSTOOD WHAT IT WAS ALL ABOUT. I ALWAYS KEPT HIDDEN THE MARITAL DIFFICULTIES THAT WE WERE GOING THROUGH.

With the divorce, Dave and I agreed together that the children would live with me full-time, and that he would be free to spend time with them whenever he wanted. Although I didn't realize it, it was at this point that each of our three children began their own journey through Oz.

It was Jordan, my oldest daughter, who tried to bring to my attention the fact that she, too, was experiencing the effects of the divorce. In my own brokenness, I just didn't get it. I thought it was different for the children. After all, they still had a mother and a father, even if they lived separately. I, on the other hand, was alone, torn from a marriage and experiencing the devastation of it all. I was such a wreck emotionally that I was barely able to keep myself together, never mind help my children. It took every ounce of energy I had to get out of bed each morning and get to work so that I could make a living and pay the bills, returning home each night trying to convince everyone that, for the most part, we were okay. At the end of the day I had nothing left to give my kids. I hated that!

I had always had everything under control. I wanted nothing more than to be a great wife, and a great mom… and now that part of my life was falling apart, too. I was helpless to hold us all together, let alone meet each individual child's specific emotional needs. In my quandary, I resolved to do what I thought was best: I urged my children to go into counseling and get help from a trained professional. My youngest daughter, Grace, agreed almost immediately. Jordan's time would come later. My son, Joe, however, declined — and even with all of my persuasive skills, I couldn't get him to change his mind.

I WANTED NOTHING MORE THAN TO BE A GREAT WIFE, AND A GREAT MOM... AND NOW THAT PART OF MY LIFE WAS FALLING APART, TOO.

Now don't get me wrong: we all stuck it out together, especially in the beginning. We always had a house to come home to, food in the refrigerator, and clothes on our backs. Physically we were all in attendance, but emotionally we would go down different paths simultaneously. Jordan would go off to college. Grace would get involved in the local church. And Joe would turn to drugs.

Chapter 4

GLINDA THE GOOD

As Dorothy took in the panoramic view of the mysterious, magnificent land of Oz, she observed an opaque sphere floating towards her, descending from the sky. How awestruck we were, watching the movie as children, when from this globe appeared the beautiful Glinda. She wore the most magical dress that sparkled in the sunlight, with a jeweled crown upon her head, and a star-topped wand in her hand.

In its day, there was some controversy—at least in the Christian community—over whether or not *The Wizard of Oz* promoted witchcraft, with its positive portrayal of "Glinda the Good Witch of the North." The point being made was that it was irrelevant whether Glinda was good or bad...she was still a witch. Some concerned parents wanted the book removed from library shelves. As a child, however, I remember viewing Glinda as nothing more than a beautiful, magical princess, there to watch over Dorothy and help her find her way home.

When I watch *The Wizard of Oz* today, Glinda is a reminder to me of my personal faith in God. Dorothy was introduced to Glinda upon her arrival in Oz, at the very beginning of her journey. My awakening to God, however, took place more than twenty years prior to this devastating storm, way before my journey began.

As a young adult, just out of college and living on my own for the first time, I found myself searching for answers to some very big questions about life and its purpose. Although I wasn't brought up in a religious home and hadn't been in a church since I was a child, I was amazed to find myself turning to God in prayer — asking Him to reveal Himself to me that I might know if He truly existed. In answer to that simple but sincere request, almost immediately I found myself becoming acutely aware of God's presence in our world.

ALTHOUGH I WASN'T BROUGHT UP IN A RELIGIOUS HOME AND HADN'T BEEN IN A CHURCH SINCE I WAS A CHILD, I WAS AMAZED TO FIND MYSELF TURNING TO GOD IN PRAYER — ASKING HIM TO REVEAL HIMSELF TO ME THAT I MIGHT KNOW IF HE TRULY EXISTED.

At first, God showed me signs of His personal handiwork. The flowers around me all seemed bigger and brighter; their aroma somehow seemed sweeter. The birds in the trees sang the most beautiful musical arrangements I had ever heard.

The sky appeared bluer, the clouds whiter and fluffier than ever. For the first time, everything in nature seemed to point me to a divine Creator.

Then God showed me signs of His love through the actions of people. Suddenly I noticed those around me doing the nicest things. I sensed the love of God as I noticed a mother holding the hand of her child. Seeing a couple walking arm in arm through the park, whispering and giggling to one another, brought a smile to my face. Noticing a friend helping another friend move furniture brought hope to my soul. And seeing complete strangers exchanging kind words and polite greetings to one another made me believe anything was possible. I couldn't explain why I hadn't noticed these things before, but overnight, my focus and perspective on life had significantly changed. Somehow I was seeing things from a completely different vantage point. Could all this be a result of sincere query to God?

I continued my search and began to read the Bible. Though I had read many of the stories before, this time it was different. The printed words seemed to come alive and jump off the page at me. With every question I asked, God responded with an answer written in that Book that seemed to make perfect sense. Before I knew it, I had found satisfaction in my discovery, and I felt my pursuit of truth was complete. I bowed my head, asking God to forgive me of everything I had ever done wrong, and invited Him to be at the center of my life, guiding me from that day forward.

And some people thought Glinda was controversial! When I told my family and friends that I had begun a personal relationship with God, it definitely raised a lot of eyebrows. That's putting it mildly! They had never heard of such a thing and found it quite strange. I had no idea that asking God into my life would stir up so many emotions and elicit so many comments from the people around me.

"She must be lonely," they said. "Living away from home must be too much for her!" "What's all this talk about God and going to church so much? She's not dancing and going out to parties? It's simply not right!"

As a young adult, I just figured that if God was real and offering me a friendship with Him for life, I was going to take Him up on that. It seemed to me the deal of a lifetime, one that I simply couldn't refuse. To this day, I believe entering into this divine partnership was the most important and best decision of my life!

Glinda and Dorothy's relationship is an important one too, and a lot more spiritual than first meets the eye. Dorothy's dilemma becomes clear almost immediately upon her arrival in Oz. How is she going to get back home to Kansas? She looks at the broken down farm house. She looks at Glinda and then at Toto. "I don't think we can get back the way we came."

As I watch the movie today, I think to myself: "Come on! She arrived in a bubble from the sky. She's holding a magical wand. Can't she just wave the wand and send Dorothy home?"

I wondered the same thing after my divorce. Couldn't God could somehow wave His magic wand and turn everything back to the way things used to be? I wanted to go back to the time when things were happy instead of sad, whole instead of broken, normal instead of insane, and in control instead of chaotic. But as I pondered that thought over and over again in my mind, I realized that things hadn't been happy and whole for a long time. There had been eight years of infidelity. The first four I was totally unaware of; during the last four, the infidelity was less frequent as we attempted intermittently to work on the marriage. Nevertheless, the infidelity bred lies, and lies destroyed trust. The breakdown of trust eventually created chaos. I had not been living what I considered a "normal" life for some time.

I WANTED TO GO BACK TO THE TIME WHEN THINGS WERE HAPPY INSTEAD OF SAD, WHOLE INSTEAD OF BROKEN, NORMAL INSTEAD OF INSANE, AND IN CONTROL INSTEAD OF CHAOTIC.

I realized that my heart had been shattered, my spirit wounded, and my days filled with sadness long before the divorce. I wasn't sure how far back I had to go to see where the deception actually began. It was confusing trying to distinguish what parts of my life were genuine and which weren't. I had memories of happier times, but was it really happiness if I was happy while being deceived? Did it even matter? Did anything matter anymore? It all seemed like a joke… a big, bad joke on me.

No, I wasn't going to get home the way I came, either. I'd have to discover another way to bring back my smile, to find normalcy, to feel whole and complete, able to trust without reservation.

Glinda didn't wave her magic wand and make everything right for Dorothy. Instead she introduced Dorothy to some wonderful people, gave her important guidance and direction, granted her some special gifts to protect and empower her, then disappeared as quickly as she came — though she continued to watch over Dorothy from above, intervening when necessary.

Glinda may not have had the ability to wave her magic wand and send Dorothy back to Kansas, but we learn later that Dorothy could have gone home right then and there with the power of the magical shoes. Glinda could have told her more about the magical shoes, but she chose not to. It seems Glinda knew that there were some things Dorothy needed to learn on her journey — things she wouldn't learn by going straight home.

Journeys often change our way of looking at things. Journeys often change us. They give us opportunities to learn and grow. It's interesting, because journeys usually take us out of our comfort zone and into new and different environments. Given the choice, most of us want to return to what's familiar. But then we never experience anything new, we never learn, we never change, and we never grow.

It doesn't surprise me that Glinda didn't give Dorothy a choice. And it doesn't surprise me now that God didn't wave a magic wand in my situation, nor appear to give me much of a choice. Dorothy and I would both head home via a new direction… through the land of Oz.

The journey following my divorce would be the greatest test of my faith in my twenty-five years as a Christian. I had always thought my faith was strong. Now, however, in my post-divorce, storm-devastated condition, I found that my faith was stripped down to two basic promises which I held onto tightly. I remembered these Scriptures from my earliest days as a believer. God seemed to lock them in my mind for just this time. The first was this:

"Never will I leave you nor forsake you." (Deuteronomy 31:6)

With this promise in my heart, I never felt abandoned by God. Just as Glinda always watched Dorothy from above, I always believed that God had His eyes on me, and would intervene if necessary. I didn't doubt it for a moment!

Ever since I became a Christian, church has always been a very special place for me. Whether we're talking about the years of full-time ministry, or years when I simply attended church services and events as an active member of the congregation, I have countless, treasured memories. With the divorce, however, came a tidal wave of pain which made it very difficult for me to be involved in church the way I was accustomed. It was a constant reminder of the death of my marriage, as well as the destruction of my lifelong dream of being in full-time ministry for God. Where I used to attend several services a week, often for hours at a time, I now found I could only handle one Sunday morning service a week for about forty-five minutes. That was just enough time to enjoy a little worship, hear a good message, and finish with a prayer. It was all I was capable of before breaking down in tears. Now I spent most of my time with God in private, just Him and me.

Fortunately, I found Suncoast Community Church, a congregation whose leaders saw their church as a hospital for injured Christians. They welcomed me with open arms and ministered to me, without judgment. Although I hadn't quite understood their mission before, I know now that if it hadn't been for their ministry, I could have easily been without a church home—alone and forlorn—for a long time.

I so appreciated the love and support this new church extended me. As disconnected as my life was, it offered a much needed place of accountability. I knew I was surrounded by loving people who would help, if I needed them. Really I just needed time to heal. It was here that I also found support and guidance for my new divorced status.

What I didn't expect was the rejection I felt from many former Christian friends and leaders who didn't understand the pain I was in. Some judged my relationship with God during that time. It seemed many looked down on me assuming I had backslidden. Some just disassociated with me, not knowing how to relate, or what to do. That was okay. I understood that they didn't understand. As they moved away from me, I drew closer to God.

MORE THAN EVER, I NEEDED SOMEONE WHO WOULDN'T ABANDON ME, BUT WOULD STICK WITH ME THROUGH THIS MOST DIFFICULT PART OF MY LIFE.

Most of the time, I sensed the presence of God in my life just as strongly as ever before. I heard His voice and knew He was with me. My faith was not in the church itself or in other Christians, but in God alone. It was God who promised *never* to leave me, and I believed Him. More than ever, I needed someone who wouldn't abandon me, but would stick with me through this most difficult part of my life.

He truly showed Himself as "the friend who sticks closer than a brother." (Proverbs 18:24b)

I found out an amazing truth at this juncture. God isn't faithful to me because of my goodness or because of my faithfulness to Him. The Bible says that His name is "Faithful"—it's who He is—and He must be true to His name. Thus, when He makes a promise, He follows through on it. When God says, "Never will I leave you nor forsake you," it's based on His character, not mine. So in my brokenness and times of darkness, in my weakest place, He is still with me. What a wonderful truth!

The second promise I held close to my heart was this:

"For I know the plans I have for you, declares the Lord, plans to prosper you and not to harm you, plans to give you hope and a future." (Jeremiah 29:11)

Standing on this promise forced me to look at the larger picture. God's plan is very often made up of many dreams. And though one dream may come to an end, it often signals the beginning of the next.

Over the last twenty-five years, I have seen God do countless miracles in my life and in the lives of those around me. I know my God, and I know His voice. Life can be tough. It doesn't always go the way I'd like it to go, or the way I expect it to go. Things don't always work in my favor. People are people—sometimes they let me down. But God has never let me down. He has always been there for me. He has always walked with me through each situation, good or bad.

I do believe there is a plan—His plan—for my life. He knows it from beginning to end, and He will see me through it. I know that God's ways are not my ways, but most of the time, I think I understand pretty well what God is doing in my life. During my divorce, as I watched my dreams dissolve before me, I had to remember that I don't always see the entire picture.

I have come to realize that life was never meant to be a smooth journey. Instead, it's filled with ups and downs, the good, the bad, and the ugly. I have seen that the greatest times of my life—believe it or not—have usually followed the most difficult times. If it were up to me, I would have avoided the entire lot altogether. But God sees to it that I don't miss the lessons I need to learn. He walks with me through the difficult times, knowing there will be invaluable truths that I will discover along the way, and that great blessings await me when I get to my journey's end.

In L. Frank Baum's *The Wonderful Wizard of Oz*, the Good Witch of the North places a magical kiss upon Dorothy's forehead for protection. Dorothy doesn't realize how much power there is in this expression of her affection and favor. Neither did I understand the depth of God's favor and protection that rested upon me, as a Christian. (I'll share more about this later.)

Glinda's gifts of a special kiss and a pair of ruby slippers were critical to Dorothy's survival in Oz and safe return home. In the same way, God's presence and protection were critical to my survival; they carried me through to the place of healing and restoration in life.

Chapter 5 | MUNCHKIN LAND

The first task of Glinda the Good was to introduce the newly arrived Dorothy to the citizens of Munchkin Land. As Dorothy ventured from her house, she heard giggling, but couldn't catch a glimpse of any of the residents who ducked out of sight each time she turned in their direction. Their hats and clothing were adorned with colorful flowers and objects that blended perfectly with the environment, camouflaging them from view.

Glinda guided Dorothy toward the town's center, calling, "Come out, Come out, wherever you are, and see the young lady who fell from a star."

I remember being amazed as a child, watching the movie, as the screen was suddenly filled with a vivid cast of characters, all under four feet in height. Imagine, a whole town full of little people! How fascinating! Who had ever seen such a thing before? One by one they introduced themselves, from the mayor of Munchkin City, to the coroner, to the ballet dancers of the Lullaby League, finishing off with the tough roughkins known as the Lollipop Guild. I sat there, eyes wide open, taking it all in, and smiling in amazement.

What I didn't pick up until much later (after reading the book) was the fact that the Munchkins had been enslaved for years by the Wicked Witch of the East. Dorothy's house had fallen on the witch and killed her, breaking the powerful spell the witch had over the Munchkins, setting them free. This scene in the movie is actually a conversation between Dorothy and the Munchkins. Dorothy explains who she is and how her house happened to fall upon the wicked witch, and the Munchkins respond with a grandiose welcome and ecstatic expressions of their thankfulness!

This interesting exchange of dialogue between Dorothy and this unique community very much reminds me of my first visit to the local support group called DivorceCare. Divorce groups, in general, tend to attract a diverse array of individuals. Some attendees are young, and some are older. Some had been married only a few months or a few years; others had been married for decades. Groups may consist of all male or all female participants or they may be mixed. Often you have people who are newly separated, just divorced, or on their second or third divorce, all in the same group. My divorce group was no different. It drew its own motley crew of characters, and I was one of them. I felt I stuck out like a sore thumb with my blonde curly hair, high-heeled shoes, and corporate suit. But it was okay. The fact that I didn't know any of these people and they didn't know me only made it easier.

> MY DIVORCE GROUP WAS NO DIFFERENT. IT DREW ITS OWN MOTLEY CREW OF CHARACTERS, AND I WAS ONE OF THEM. I FELT I STUCK OUT LIKE A SORE THUMB WITH MY BLONDE CURLY HAIR, HIGH-HEELED SHOES, AND CORPORATE SUIT.

Moments after I first arrived, I found myself staring at the coordinator like a deer in headlights. She said a lot of interesting things, I'm sure, but I didn't hear any of them. As she was talking, all I could think about was how I was going to tell her that I had made a mistake, that this just wasn't for me, and that maybe I would come back some other time. I was petrified!

You may wonder, "Why did you even go in the first place?"

It was only weeks after the divorce, and I was alone and floundering. I had been sitting in church one Sunday morning, when they announced that the divorce group was starting up again for a new ten-week course. I was so numb at the time that I wasn't hearing much of anything, but amazingly, I sensed God whispering in my soul: "You need to go! It will help you." In one sense it was a whisper; then again, it had the impact of an announcement made over a loudspeaker. I obeyed and went.

But before that first meeting began, I was already trying to wiggle my way out of the entire experience. I was truly scared to death, so much so that I couldn't seem to get the words out of my mouth. The lovely lady who met me at the door ushered me to a seat in the circle.

For the first few weeks, I didn't say anything other than my name. I nodded my head a few times, but I was much too afraid to talk. I knew that if I said anything, I'd start to cry. Once the tears started, I would never be able to stop them. Losing control like that was not something I was comfortable with, therefore I just had to hold it all in!

I KNEW THAT IF I SAID ANYTHING, I'D START TO CRY. ONCE THE TEARS STARTED, I WOULD NEVER BE ABLE TO STOP THEM.

Every week, the group leaders showed a half-hour video. These videos covered everything that people go through during separation and divorce. They were vital to me because they showed me that I wasn't alone in many of the things I was experiencing—in fact, I was often a "textbook" case. There were things that I felt guilty about that I learned were actually unavoidable after-effects I shouldn't be ashamed of. Where I thought I had permanent scars, I discovered my wounds could be treated with counseling. I returned to the group again and again because I found these videos so interesting and informative. I wanted to see more.

The group leaders also gave me a book to read during the week that reinforced the instruction in the videos. It was part workbook, part journal, and it helped me to relate the material to my personal situation. In class I wrote down things I didn't want to forget. During the week, I answered the workbook questions, going at my own pace.

At the weekly meetings, we always took time to go around the circle and give everyone a few minutes to talk, if they wanted to, or share a prayer request. Although we were all very different, in one way we were the same. We were all going through a really tough time. In that circle, our differences didn't seem recognizable. Our coming together each week seemed to strengthen us. I grew to really like the group, and everyone in it.

Eventually, I opened up and began to talk, too. I found that I needed to release the tears and the pain that were bottled up inside of me. To my surprise, my tears didn't go on forever; letting them go brought me some much-needed relief. In the divorce group setting, there was nobody I needed to impress. There was also no one who would judge me. Sometimes you can't tell everything to your family, friends, or coworkers. They might be frightened or anxious and worry about your well-being. They might wonder if you are stable enough to be working. It's often better to vent with people that you don't know so well, and who aren't involved in your everyday life, yet understand the intensity of your situation. The divorce group did just that. Every week we would listen to one another, offer encouragement, and lift up one another in prayer.

Being the private person I was, I was surprised that I could open up the way I did. But the divorce group turned out to be exactly where I needed to be at that time. It was a good experience and got me started on my journey to healing. Just as God had said, it helped me—a lot!

There was one lesson from the group that I had to learn the hard way. One of the first recommendations I heard in those videos was that for every five years you have been married, you should allow at least one year before you consider remarrying. You should use the time to focus on getting your life back on track, healing, and rediscovering yourself as a single person. For me, that meant that I should not even think about remarrying for at least four years. On top of that, we weren't supposed to date anyone while going through the ten-week divorce group program. When I came into the divorce group, dating was the farthest thing from my mind. I couldn't foresee that even being an issue. During the third or fourth week, however, Sam joined the group. Lo and behold, in a short period of time, we started dating.

At the beginning, Sam was like the Good Samaritan to me. He found me pretty beat up by the divorce, withering away, and in an awful state of mind. I had completely lost my appetite and had withdrawn from all of my normal physical and social activities. All I did was go to work and come home. Eating very little, I lost a lot of weight, dropping three dress sizes, and my family and friends were starting to worry. Of course as women, we all think it's great to be thin, but it had gotten well beyond that.

Sam was a physical trainer. He offered to put me on an exercise program and assist me in developing a healthy meal plan. We started spending a lot of time working out together. Knowing I hadn't eaten all day, Sam would prepare small meals and persuade me to eat them by reminding me that if I didn't, I wouldn't have the energy to workout. We became friends and ended up spending a lot of time doing fun things together. I grew physically stronger and our relationship gave me more self-confidence than I had had in a long time. Sam was a romantic, and I had never really had anyone shower me with so much attention before. I felt like I was falling in love.

For a while this relationship distracted me from how broken I was inside. During the day, while we were out having fun, everything seemed great! But as I drove home at night, alone with my thoughts, I realized that I was just trying to avoid dealing with reality. Looking at my life, I realized there was significant storm damage that needed attention—things that needed repair, both in myself, and in my family. Some days I drove home wondering whether or not I should check myself into an institution. I thought about what that might entail. On Fridays, after work, I often wondered if I would make it through to Monday, or if this would be the weekend I'd completely lose my mind. Sam wasn't aware of my mental torment... no one was. On a couple of occasions, I tried to explain it to him, but it didn't seem to register, so I retreated.

Sam wanted to move forward into a serious, committed relationship, but I knew I was incapable of doing that. The relationship we had was a great escape, but deep down, I knew I needed more than that. I needed some serious help. I wasn't ready for any type of committed relationship. I had work to do. I had a journey to go on. I needed to leave Munchkin Land, get to the Emerald City, and find the Wizard. Maybe the Wizard could help me find my way home to wholeness.

THAT'S WHAT THIS JOURNEY THROUGH OZ WOULD BE ALL ABOUT FOR ME: A JOURNEY OF SELF-DISCOVERY, HEALING AND RESTORATION.

In turning away from Sam and moving forward on the path that lay ahead, I was making a decision to follow the guidance I should have heeded from the start. I was going to work on rebuilding myself and my life again, from the inside out. I would find the support people who could assist me in doing that. That's what this journey through Oz would be all about for me: a journey of self-discovery, healing and restoration. I knew it would take time, focus, and energy. So I decided not to actively pursue any dating relationships.

I've learned that when you first rebound after a lengthy, committed relationship, you need to be on your guard! Important decisions that affect the rest of your life should be avoided during emotionally, unstable times. My relationship with Sam lasted a little less than a year. There were moments when I was laughing, smiling, and enjoying life again. It seemed wonderful. I could easily have ended up in a new marriage that I now know would have quickly failed. From the beginning, I had said that I didn't know if this relationship was just meant for now, for a little longer, or forever. When you're on the rebound, it's easy to think right away that it's forever. It took about six or seven months for my emotions to calm down, so that I could see clearly. Then it took me several more months to untangle myself from a relationship that I realized wasn't going anywhere. It made me sad to discover that my feelings had led me astray. But it would have been so much worse to discover that after entering into another marriage. Lesson learned: Be cautious!

Chapter 6 | THE RUBY SLIPPERS

As the evil Wicked Witch of the West leaned over the legs of her dead sister to remove the ruby slippers from her feet, the shoes disappeared in an instant! The striped stockings curled up from toe to ankle, and the dead witch's legs were sucked under the floorboards of what was left of Dorothy's flying house. Shocked, the Wicked Witch of the West turned toward Dorothy and Glinda, only to find that the precious footwear she wanted to claim for herself was now fitted securely on Dorothy's feet. Glinda whispered to Dorothy to keep those shoes on her feet at all times. There must be a strong magic associated with them for the Wicked Witch to want them so badly.

Many people don't realize that in the original story of *The Wizard of Oz*, the magical shoes were actually silver. The moviemakers wanted to show off the newly-developed Technicolor—so the silver shoes in Baum's book became a magnificent ruby red. I have always been fascinated by Dorothy's fancy footwear. To me, those ruby slippers have come to symbolize the constant presence and power of God in my life as a Christian.

Whether you picture them red or silver, these magical shoes were the best possible choice of footwear for Dorothy's journey. They were of good construction, high quality, fit perfectly and looked great. And they had this mysterious power associated with them. Even to this day, I remember quite vividly the scene in the movie, where the camera moved in for a close up of Dorothy's feet. She adjusted her stance in the glimmering sunlight, as she modeled the bow-topped ruby slippers. I watched in awe, enchanted by their beauty and curious about their magic.

In the book, we're told that Dorothy arrived in Oz in a pair of old, worn-out shoes, typical of a farm girl in Kansas in the early 1900s. If she were to set out on her journey across the yellow brick road with inadequate footwear, surely it would result in injury and despair. Dorothy didn't think much of the silver shoes upon receipt. In fact, she nicely took them and put them aside. When it came time to set out beyond the boundaries of Munchkin Land, however, Dorothy went back and examined the shoes more carefully and found them to be much more appropriate for the long trip ahead. She put them on her feet, discarded the others, and set out on her journey. She really had no idea of the power that they possessed and how important they would be to her ultimate goal of getting back to Kansas.

When I arrived in Oz, it wasn't my shoes that were worn out—it was me. With as little strength as I had left, the journey should have ended before it got started. But it didn't. Something in me was determined to find wholeness and life again. Though I certainly wasn't filled with enthusiasm, excitement or energy, I knew that I was filled with God's Spirit, and somehow, God would get me where I needed to be. I figured nothing could be worse than where I was now. So off I started.

THOUGH I CERTAINLY WASN'T FILLED WITH ENTHUSIASM, EXCITEMENT OR ENERGY, I KNEW THAT I WAS FILLED WITH GOD'S SPIRIT, AND SOMEHOW, GOD WOULD GET ME WHERE I NEEDED TO BE.

Like Dorothy, I had no idea what lay ahead for me in my travels... but God did. He saw to it that I was perfectly equipped by giving me His Holy Spirit. Understand that God's Spirit is anything but ordinary. His Spirit is packed with power, wisdom, protection, and so much more. When God decides to clothe you in His Spirit, you can take on any task, any journey, any battle before you. With God's Spirit the ordinary is transformed into the extraordinary. The Bible tells us that in Old Testament times, God's Spirit came upon ordinary, everyday people and transformed them into powerful prophets, mighty warriors, courageous kings and queens.

Dorothy's power was hidden in her shoes, but mine was hidden in my heart. Both would be revealed in due time.

The ruby slippers alerted others that although Dorothy looked like an average girl, there was something different about her—something special. The Wicked Witch recognized Dorothy's power when she saw those shoes on her feet. The ruby slippers also caught the attention of the Wizard's assistant in the Emerald City. Very quickly, he granted her an audience with the Wizard.

The Scripture describes God's people as having "the seal of the Spirit" upon them—that the presence of God's Spirit in their lives marks them as belonging to Him. It changes how they are viewed by others and what they are capable of doing. So how can we know if the Holy Spirit is within us? Dorothy's slippers were eye-catching, bold and brightly colored! God's Spirit, on the other hand, is invisible to the human eye. But if we look closely, we can see evidence of His existence in our lives.

"The fruit of the Spirit is love, joy, peace, patience, kindness, goodness, faithfulness, gentleness and self-control." (Galatians 5:22-23)

Nobody is perfect, but I've always believed that a person filled with God's Spirit will make good choices more often than not, resist the temptation to do things God says are off limits, and try to do things that honor Him. At this point I had to ask myself what evidence I had that God's Spirit was living within me.

For years I had consciously chosen to live within God's boundaries, consistently making the choices I thought would please Him. But these days, I felt my attitude and my actions were falling short of my own standards—let alone God's. In my heartache, I couldn't always manage to put on a happy face. (That God-given joy didn't seem apparent.) There were times I lost my temper and flew off the handle at people. (What about gentleness, patience, and self-control? …not so evident here.) At the suggestion of my doctor, I was taking prescription drugs to manage my depression. As a Christian, I had always been so anti-drug, yet now I felt I had no choice in the matter. I simply couldn't function without the medication. It was my only option as I sought therapy. Then each evening, I found continued relief from my anxiety and stress in a glass of wine.

I realize that to many people, this wouldn't sound at all unusual or alarming or unacceptable. But these behaviors were completely contrary to the way I'd lived my life for twenty years. It distressed me personally. It wasn't so much that I cared about what people thought, as I was concerned it would be written off by many as mere hypocrisy on my part! Truth be told, I wasn't trying to be rebellious. I was just trying to hang on to my life. I just wanted to feel normal again and there didn't seem to be a quick, cut-and-dry answer for that. I grasped wildly for solutions and sometimes they were not the best choices for me, and I found that out the hard way. I resolved that until I could figure it all out for myself, I'd just do my best to keep my questionable actions under cover. I knew eventually things would come into proper balance again.

It's funny how you can be so strong and firm and immovable on something your whole life, and then suddenly your perspective changes forever.

IT'S FUNNY HOW YOU CAN BE SO STRONG AND FIRM AND IMMOVABLE ON SOMETHING YOUR WHOLE LIFE, AND THEN SUDDENLY YOUR PERSPECTIVE CHANGES FOREVER.

You may think that condemnation set in, as my conscience got the best of me. But that's not what happened at all! Instead of focusing on my lack of good choices, I felt that God's Spirit brought something else to the forefront of my mind. I realized how judgmental of others I had been in the past, when I was strong, and they were weak. Many times I had thought to myself, "If he just read his Bible more, he'd be stronger" or "If she just came to church more, life would be better" In reality, people were hurting, confused and struggling, and at the time, I just didn't get it! In the back of my mind I always had some glib response. I was thinking, "They just aren't trying hard enough. Or they're not following God's rules, and that's why they're in this mess." In my immaturity, I thought I had all the answers. What I didn't see then was that I lacked compassion.

Thinking of this now made me sick to my stomach. How could I have been so ignorant? So insensitive? So completely clueless? At this point, it seemed that God thought it more important for me to learn this life-changing lesson than to beat myself up over a glass of wine.

This is when I began to learn the meaning of the word *grace*. I had heard it many times in many sermons and I had thought I understood it, but something was missing from my definition. Perhaps it was the personal and practical application of it.

Through the struggles I faced in my journey through Oz, the many times I stumbled and fell, I experienced God's grace in a whole new way. He wasn't *only* with me when I made the right choices and did the right things—He was with me when I didn't and couldn't. He was with me when I felt like I had it all together, and He was with me when I was a miserable, helpless mess.

God knows me better than I know myself. When I'm struggling with life, He not only sees my struggle, He understands the reason why—even when I don't! I have found God to be patient and kind, loving and forgiving, right there with me every step of the way. He was always whispering that there were better days ahead. He never pushed me or moved ahead without me. He waited with me and walked with me at my pace. He gently helped me get where I needed to be. I know now that we can't change the world by trying to change other people. We change the world by letting God change us.

I KNOW NOW THAT WE CAN'T CHANGE THE WORLD BY TRYING TO CHANGE OTHER PEOPLE. WE CHANGE THE WORLD BY LETTING GOD CHANGE US.

In *The Wizard of Oz*, it turns out that the mysterious magical shoes have the power to transport anyone who wears them anywhere they desire. At the end of Dorothy's journey, it is the power of her shoes that return her to Kansas. The power of God's Spirit within me did so much more.

First and foremost, God's Spirit was the catalyst that set me in motion to live and not die. God is the source of all life; His Spirit is the fire that fuels us, refusing to allow us to give up on our destiny. After going through the storm of Divorce, all my hope and strength, my desire to live had been depleted. Yet the flicker of God's Spirit within me miraculously sparked the strength I needed to pick myself up again. It gave me the vision necessary to believe that something better was ahead for me. I wasn't capable of this on my own—I had nothing left. God did it all!

God's Spirit was also what drove me throughout my journey. This fire, that for a time barely flickered in my soul, moved me to find answers that would ultimately bring healing and wholeness to my life. Every day, God's Spirit coaxed me from my bed to get out and into the world, moving forward regardless of life's difficulties. Every day, I faced another hurdle, but God's Spirit lifted me over each one.

The Holy Spirit provided guidance. Many times when I would have turned this way or that, I sensed that He wanted me to take a different direction. I followed that divine instinct time and time again, believing that it was God's leading. I was continually amazed, that with no roadmap, I so often found myself in the right place at the right time, meeting the right people. Eventually I found the Wizard who showed me the way home to normalcy.

In my humblest state, God revealed to me, through His Spirit, these important lessons. In the dark and empty places, I caught a glimpse of how things looked through God's eyes. I was faced with the most profound truths that have changed me forever. This has given me an even greater reverence and respect for God and His ways. Truly the Spirit of God showed Himself to be my Teacher.

As I journeyed through Oz, the Spirit of God journeyed with me. It was a comfort to me, as if I had my own magical shoes — or rather, "spiritual shoes" — snuggly upon my feet. They never came off. In tired and lonely times, I felt comforted from the inside out. In scary times, I felt divinely protected. In times of confusion, I felt as if wisdom and direction were dropped into my lap. What an amazing experience!

Dorothy's shoes didn't come with instructions, and for most of her time in Oz she didn't understand their power. I didn't always comprehend how the power of God worked in my life either. One of the most important discoveries I made on my journey was a greater acknowledgement of my role and responsibilities in this divine relationship. I don't control or manipulate God's Spirit to make Him work for me. I don't consult a manual to determine how and when to "use" Him. I walk with God, look for His presence, fellowship with Him, and follow His direction. He is the Leader and I am the follower.

I WALK WITH GOD, LOOK FOR HIS PRESENCE, FELLOWSHIP WITH HIM, AND FOLLOW HIS DIRECTION. HE IS THE LEADER AND I AM THE FOLLOWER.

The friendship and companionship of God, through the presence of the Holy Spirit, is a remarkable thing. We were never intended to go through life totally disconnected from our Creator. Just as Adam and Eve walked in the Garden with God, we can walk and talk with God, too. It is a priceless gift He offers freely to every one of us. When we receive God's Spirit, we receive His wisdom and guidance. We have access to His love and His peace. In times of need, He provides. In times of sickness, He heals. He is everything we need to be complete and whole—capable not just of finishing this journey called Life, but doing it in an extraordinary fashion.

"I have come that you might have life and have it to the full." (John 10:10)

God has already given us physical life. He so wants us to take it to the next level… He wants us to seek Him and find in Him spiritual life, as well.

"You will seek Me and find Me when you seek Me with all your heart. I will be found by you,' declares the Lord." (Jeremiah 29:13-14)

Years ago, I wondered if God was real and if there was a purpose for my life. That led to a simple prayer of asking

God to reveal Himself to me. He followed through on my request, convincing me that He was, in fact, real. In my new spiritual understanding, I responded by faith. I believed what my soul whispered was true. I asked God to forgive me of my wrongdoings in the past, and in turn I decided to trust in Him for each day of my life, and then after. What a relief that was! It was one thing knowing that God was out there, somewhere, but now I realized He was here, too, in my everyday life, with me.

When we respond to God's invitation, He pours His power into us, giving us the ability to live far above and beyond an ordinary life. Through this partnership with the Holy Spirit, we see God moving in miraculous ways, touching not only our lives but the lives of those around us. Wow! When I first sought God, when I responded to His invitation and connected with Him, I had no idea how much it would mean to me—that such a simple prayer would change my life forever. And even today, simple prayers just like mine, continue to be whispered to God, and He continues to respond in like fashion.

Chapter 7

FOLLOW THE YELLOW BRICK ROAD

By this time, the goal for both Dorothy and I was to get home. Dorothy wanted nothing more than to get back to that place of familiarity to see her Aunt Em and Uncle Henry. In the same way, I was believing to find that comfortable dwelling place of wholeness, stability, and normalcy once more.

Glinda informed Dorothy that her best shot at achieving that was to set out to see the Wizard. Surely he would be able to assist her. The Wizard lived in the Emerald City, which Dorothy would find by following a road paved with yellow bricks that ran throughout the Land of Oz. The directions seemed easy enough. But just in case, each of the Munchkins reminds her: "Follow the Yellow Brick Road. Follow the Yellow Brick Road. Follow the Yellow Brick Road."

In the movie, the camera focused on Dorothy's feet in those beautiful ruby slippers, as she took her first step. A delicate and delightful tune began to play, as she took another step, and then another. Slowly she moved forward. The song picked up its tempo, her step quickened, and the Munchkin choir sang in full voice, as she skipped off toward the horizon. She stopped for a moment at the city limits, turned around, and waved goodbye. Her journey had begun.

My sendoff was a little bit different. I didn't have a movie studio with a million dollar budget behind me, so there were no Munchkins to cheer me on. No music, no singing, no smiling or waving. No encouraging words. No nothing. Just my decision to move forward and find the help I needed.

FOR ME, EACH DAY WOULD START WITH A STEP.

Unfortunately, I wasn't even sure what kind of help I needed, so a map was irrelevant, let alone a yellow brick road. I didn't have ruby slippers, but I did have the Holy Spirit within me. I was confident He would guide and direct my path. The Scripture says:

"A man's steps are directed by the Lord." (Proverbs 20:24)

Dorothy started her adventure with a single step. For me, each day would start with a step. Some days it was a baby step here, a long pause, and then another step there. Other days there would be several steps. It was some time before the pace picked up to the point where there was consistent forward momentum.

Watching *The Wizard of Oz* on television, I remember that at each commercial break, there would be a reprise of one of two songs: "We're Off to See the Wizard" or "Follow the Yellow Brick Road." They were delightful songs, that as a child, I never tired of hearing.

In real life, however, the songs that played over and over in my head were harder to listen to. The first one sounded like this:

Ok Gail, that's your alarm ringing. Come on. Wake up.
Reach over and shut that alarm off. That's it.
Now open your eyes. You can do that. Come on. Open your eyes.
There you go.
Now let's get you out of this bed. You can do that.
Flip over the blanket. Come on, flip over the blanket. That's it.
Now, sit up. Come on, Gail, you've got to sit up.
You can't stay down. You've got to sit up.
That's it! Come on. You can do it. There you go.
You did it!
Ok, let's get those legs over the side of the bed. That's right.
Now put your feet onto the floor. Excellent!
Stand and move straight to the shower. No stopping.
Once you're in that shower you'll be fine.
That's it! You did it!

Every morning, without fail, that same tune would play over and over again, and I would obey. I had to talk myself through every step. Once I got to the shower I was okay.

The rest I could do. Sometimes I'd struggle a little bit at the mirror, getting dressed and putting on my makeup, but most of the time I could manage.

Then I'd get to the office, and the second song would begin:

Okay Gail, here you are at work. You can do this.
All you have to do is get out of the car and into the office and you'll be good to go for the whole day. Come on now.
You can do this.
Shut off the car. That's right.
Now undo the seatbelt. There you go. Open the door.
Go ahead. That's right. Now swing your legs out the door.
Come on. Don't hesitate. You can do this. It's going to be okay.
Things always go well at work.
Don't cry. Come on, now. You can't do this now.
Look in the mirror. Get out your hanky. Wipe away those tears.
It will be okay.
Where's the Visine? You've made your eyes all red.
Okay, put your head back. There you go.
Those drops will take away the redness. That's okay.
Take a deep breath. It's going to be alright. Take another breath.
God will help you. You're going to make it. Ready?
Come on now. Don't start thinking about it all.
You'll just start crying again.
You can do this. Come on. Put on a smile. You can do it.
Push the door back open. That's it. Show time! Legs out.
You did it!
Straight for the door! Good Girl! Get right to your office. Focus.
No thinking about all that stuff.

What's on your agenda today?
Let's get that computer on and look at what's on the calendar.
It's going to be a busy day! It's going to be a good day!

Somehow, I made it to work everyday. I didn't miss one day due to the struggles I faced during the divorce! Some days it took a little longer to get inside than others. Some days I had to take a detour to the restroom to redo my makeup. But once I was in that office, I was okay. It was safe there. The pain and the tragedy of the whole ordeal stayed outside the building. From 8:00 am to 6:30 pm, I would meet with clients and lose myself in my work. I don't believe that my colleagues were aware of how difficult life was for me then. Like Judy Garland in her portrayal of Dorothy, I turned in an Oscar-winning performance!

Thinking about the Munchkins' instructions to "Follow the Yellow Brick Road," I am reminded of how important that message is. Just as Dorothy had to heed its directions to get to her destination, so did I. If either of us hadn't taken that first step—and then the next and the next—we would still be back in Munchkin Land.

A brick, regardless of its color, is about the size of a baby step. At first that's all I could take, baby steps. It took about twenty-five baby steps to get me from my bed to the shower each morning. It took another forty baby steps to get me from my car into my office each day. Those steps, even though they were small, were significant. Some people in my divorce group spoke of not even being able to get out of bed for weeks. I thought myself fortunate.

ONE FOOT IN FRONT OF THE OTHER, ONE STEP AT A TIME, ONE DAY AT A TIME, THAT'S HOW YOU MAKE IT WHEN THE JOURNEY IS ROUGH.

One foot in front of the other, one step at a time, one day at a time, that's how you make it when the journey is rough. My path would be difficult for a long time. Once I got to see the Wizard, the pace would pick up a bit. There would still be times, however, where the road would be rocky, and I would be confronted with some real dangers and difficulties. Sometimes I would take one step forward and two or three steps backwards. But I'd just keep on keeping on. Eventually I'd find friends who would be there to encourage me when I needed it most.

On a few occasions, I was forced to stand my ground and hold on tightly to my faith, lest I be blown away. But as soon as I could, I'd have to get moving again. I would hear the Holy Spirit whisper: "Come on. Don't stop now. Keep going. Just one more step. You can do it…" In other words, "Follow the Yellow Brick Road. Follow the Yellow Brick Road."

It worked for Dorothy. It had become my theme song as well.

Chapter 8 | TRAVELING COMPANIONS

As Dorothy made her way to the Emerald City, she gathered together a group of traveling companions. At first they were all strangers, each of them unique with their own baggage and idiosyncrasies. They weren't perfect, but they made a good team as they worked to achieve a common goal.

When you're on a long journey, it's great to have a traveling companion or two. Time goes by a little quicker when you have someone to talk to. If a problem arises and you need to think things through, two heads are better than one. In discouraging times, one person can lift up the spirit of the other. And though one traveling alone may be weak, there is strength in numbers.

In some situations we may feel that it's easier to just go it alone. (Have you ever found a group project to be a disaster?) Teams don't always work well. Some people don't pull their weight; others have personalities that lead to bickering and conflict. Who needs the drama? But although heading out on your own may seem simpler, isolation can lead to grave consequences. An individual can get distracted or lose perspective, where a group can help members stay on track. When obstacles arise, it's easier for an individual traveler to become discouraged and give up. Sometimes we need the help of others to accomplish what we're trying to get done. Individually, we may not have all the know-how, skills, monies, and contacts to get the task completed on our own.

SOMETIMES WE NEED THE HELP OF OTHERS TO ACCOMPLISH WHAT WE'RE TRYING TO GET DONE. INDIVIDUALLY, WE MAY NOT HAVE ALL THE KNOW-HOW, SKILLS, MONIES, AND CONTACTS TO GET THE TASK COMPLETED ON OUR OWN.

Determined to maintain a positive attitude, Dorothy's crew sang merrily as they skipped along arm-in-arm, down the road destined for them. Each of them hoped that, ultimately, their journey would lead them to what they were searching for. As time went on, however, they faced many challenges. It was in their greatest difficulties that their hidden gifts and talents emerged. Baum's original book gives a much more detailed description of the adventures that Dorothy and her new friends encountered. When the Wicked Witch sent a pack of wolves to eat them, the Tin Man protected them with his axe. When the Witch discharged a flock of crows to poke their eyes out, the Scarecrow shielded them from the attack. When the Witch commissioned her soldiers, the Winkies, to destroy them all, the Lion terrified them with his roar. The Winkies retreated in fear. Needless to say, through these crises, the troop of travelers bonded and became close friends.

Dorothy's team included three very interesting characters: the Scarecrow, the Tin Man, and the Cowardly Lion. The Scarecrow complained of not having a brain, yet his wisdom and intelligence guided them throughout their travels. The Tin Man insisted that he had no heart, yet he performed many kind and loving deeds. With the opportunity to confront his fears, the Cowardly Lion became the King of the Jungle he was meant to be.

I, also, had three traveling companions throughout my journey. One I think of as my Scarecrow, SK. He is highly intelligent. In my case, the Tin Man was a Tin Woman I'll refer to as TW. She has a heart of gold. And yes, there was a Lion; he is very brave.

Dorothy would never have made it through Oz, had it not been for her three comrades in arms, and neither would I. Our journey together was amazing, because the situations we faced brought out the wonderful attributes of each person. Not only did I survive the journey, I had the privilege of discovering these three incredible individuals who would become my closest of friends.

Chapter 9 | THE SCARECROW

Dorothy's journey had just begun. After a few miles down the road, she stopped to rest. Little did she realize that she was about to meet one of her closest friends in Oz. (We just never know what awaits us, around the corner each day!) Dorothy sat down at the side of the road and looked up at a funny-looking scarecrow stuck on a pole in a field. He winked at her! Kansas scarecrows didn't wink. She moved closer to take a better look and found that this man of straw was also able to speak. They carried on a delightful conversation, and when she learned that he didn't like being stuck up on the pole, she helped him down. The Scarecrow told Dorothy of his troubles. He had been put together without a brain, and that grieved him. Dorothy and the Scarecrow decided to travel to the Emerald City together. Perhaps the Wizard could give the Scarecrow a brain, as well as help Dorothy get home to Kansas. It was worth a try.

When I first moved to Florida, I met my Scarecrow—SK—at work. He was a colleague in my office. There were no winks of affection from this Scarecrow. He was a very serious, focused, no-nonsense businessman. Others looked up to him and admired him, not only for his accomplishments, but for his character and intelligence. Honestly, I found him to be very intimidating. As a new employee, I just did my best to stay out of his way.

After I'd been on the job a few months, SK was assigned to mentor me. He wasn't quite so scary, once I got to know him. Just as Dorothy did with her Scarecrow, I entered into a delightful dialogue with him and over time we became very good friends.

I had left my divorce group and was headed down my own yellow brick road when I stumbled upon SK. He ended up traveling with me through much of my journey through Oz. I couldn't have asked for a better companion. Why our paths crossed the way they did, I don't know. People find themselves in Oz for all sorts of reasons; regardless, we walked many miles together. In fact, of all my traveling companions, SK was with me the longest. His steady support was crucial to my survival.

At the beginning of my journey, I often felt like I was drowning. The weight of life seemed to push me down again and again. I latched onto SK like a life preserver, to stay afloat. He never pushed me away, although I know I was quite needy at times. SK promised to be there for me and he was. He stayed true to his word.

Everything in my life had crumbled and fallen apart. It was extremely important for me to find some stability, some consistency. Every day when I came to work, I made it a point to stop by SK's office to say hello. Every day I would find him there, returning my greeting. Somehow I took strength from that daily, unchanging routine.

For the first time in my life, I didn't have anyone to call in the case of an emergency. My family and close friends were all far away. I found it unnerving having no name for people to call if something were to happen to me. It wasn't that I was overly needy, but there's a certain sense of security in knowing that someone has your back. I discovered SK was willing to help me in anyway he could. One time, all the lights in my house suddenly went out. In a panic, I called him and he came over right away. Like many scarecrows, he wasn't very good at fixing things, but I'd have to give him an "A" for effort. It turned out to be a problem that affected the entire community, one that required the assistance of the local power company to resolve it. We had a good laugh about that later.

Great friendships are never one-sided, and neither was this one. SK and I definitely had some things in common. When I came to Florida, I left a large church community and all my friends and family behind. SK had been here only a little longer than me. He, too, had left a large church community and all of his friends and family behind. He was just as new and alone as I was. I was grieving the loss of my twenty-year marriage. He was grieving the loss of his beloved grandmother. Soon after, he would lose his grandfather and

I would lose my Dad. With no other close friends nearby, we empathized with each other, shared our thoughts and memories, and prayed for one another.

THE ROAD WE TRAVELED WAS LONG AND DIFFICULT. THERE WERE MANY POTHOLES AND UPTURNED BRICKS. BUT WE STUCK TOGETHER.

SK wasn't a particularly social person. Like many scarecrows, he would have been quite content being in his own pasture, left to himself. But I desperately needed a friend. I found my cooking skills to be very handy in opening the door of fellowship with him. Where many would never have made it thorough his front door, those homemade meatballs did it every time! Sharing a meal together gave us the opportunity to engage in much-needed conversation, keeping both of us from isolating ourselves from the world, and sinking into a deeper depression.

The road we traveled was long and difficult. There were many potholes and upturned bricks. But we stuck together. I'll never forget the night I had a bad reaction to some prescription medication. I went out after work to enjoy a glass or two of wine with some friends. It never even occurred to me to think about the possible "interactions." When I realized that something was wrong, I excused myself and left the restaurant. By the time I got to my car, I was so sick, I knew I was incapable of driving anywhere. It was getting dark and I was scared. I called SK. He came to me and stayed with me, until I was able to go home. Puking for three hours non-stop is less than admirable! He said he'd never seen someone so sick. It put me out of commission for several days.

While that was one of my lowest moments, our journey together did have some highlights. The pinnacle was an amazing gala sponsored by our company, at which we were to be the spokespeople. SK agreed to escort me to this marvelous event that included a red carpet (complete with flashing cameras), a wonderful dinner, and an amazing operatic performance. One of the advantages of my weight loss was that I could fit into almost anything. I found the most exquisite designer gown and had my hair and makeup done at the salon. The celebration was spectacular, and I felt like the belle of the ball. Almost dream-like, it was the most magical moment of my life! Of course the Scarecrow would describe it much differently. This event was my highlight, not his.

The yellow brick road led us through the darkest of valleys, to the highest of mountaintops. There were times when each one of us stumbled and fell. We picked each other up off the ground and encouraged each other to keep going. Many a tear was wiped away by my friend, the Scarecrow. Many words of encouragement were exchanged between us. Through all the tragedies and the triumphs, a unique and lasting friendship emerged that to this day, I am very thankful for.

Much of the journey was dark and difficult for the both of us, but in the midst, God was still there. SK loves music. Sometimes he would play his saxophone and I would listen.

Sometimes he would play music on the stereo, and share with me why it was so important to him. We would often talk about how God had gifted some people with incredible musical talent, and how powerfully inspiring that was.

Sometimes we attended church together. Other times we just talked about God and what the Bible has to say about things. I often wondered if God had sent my Scarecrow to me to be my friend at this critical time in my life. For if there was one underlying current in our friendship, it was that we continually reminded each other to have hope in God.

Looking back, there are many things that I gleaned from the Scarecrow. SK didn't talk a lot; following his example, I learned to be quiet. I gained a new understanding of the world by sitting back, listening and observing. I always thought that everyone saw things the same way I saw them, and interpreted them the same way I interpreted them. On many occasions, it was apparent that SK viewed things from a very different vantage point than mine. This was enlightening. It gave me a whole new understanding of how other people perceive and receive things that happen in their lives.

I'm not sure what wisdom, if any, the Scarecrow gathered from me. I regret the fact that while in Oz, the Scarecrow only knew Gail, the weak and vulnerable. I know that SK would often keep watch over me from afar. He would caution me to be careful in how I presented myself to the public eye. Between my shattered heart and the continual changes of medication, it wasn't difficult for me to appear a bit scatter-brained at times. SK knew that wasn't the real me, and didn't want others to assume it was. This Scarecrow never knew the pre-Oz Gail—strong, smart, confident, and passionate. Underneath all the chaos and catastrophe, though, he did see my heart and my hopes and dreams for the future. He knew I loved God and desperately wanted to fulfill His purpose for my life. I look forward to and trust that one day, outside of Oz, my Scarecrow will be able to say, "Wow! Gail surely got the victory and God got the glory!"

Chapter 10 | THE TIN WOMAN

Dorothy grew hungry, as she and the Scarecrow walked along the path. To get some apples off of some very grumpy trees, the Scarecrow began making faces at them. Sure enough, the trees began hurling the apples at them like cannon balls. As Dorothy crawled around picking up the apples, she happened upon something very unusual: a man made of tin, standing straight and tall and still as a statue, with an axe in his hand and an oil can nearby.

Dorothy and the Scarecrow discovered that this unique individual needed oiling in order to speak. Dorothy moved quickly with a squirt here and a squirt there, to get his lips moving. Once he was able to talk, the Tin Man revealed that he had been standing there in that very place, unable to move, for a very long time. The rain had rusted his joints. So Dorothy and the Scarecrow took turns carefully oiling each one. Life and movement returned to the Tin Man's body.

How fun it was to watch him as he clunked out a tap dance in full armor, even tooting the funnel cap upon his head in a spectacular fashion. Although he was grateful to be free, the Tin Man was not happy. He had been created without a heart. Dorothy convinced him to join her and the Scarecrow to ask for help from the Wizard of Oz.

I, too, had a second traveling companion that I refer to as TW — my Tin Woman. Just like the original Tin Man, I found that TW had a heart of gold and would do just about anything to help someone in need.

TW and I worked for the same company; we were two of the three women in an office full of men. You might have thought that, considering those numbers, TW and I would have bonded right away. But from the moment we were introduced, we both seemed to realize that we had opposite personalities. We automatically steered clear of each other to avoid any potential conflict. Several years passed and we still barely knew each other. That would change.

One morning, during the time when I was separated from my husband, TW showed up in my office. It was obvious that she was very upset. She sat down, on the verge of tears, and explained that she was going to tell me something that — if the tables were turned — she would want me to tell her. Several of our coworkers had bumped into my husband while out on the town that weekend. They had seen him in the company of another woman, with whom he was openly and obviously physically affectionate.

I took a deep breath and asked TW if she was sure about this. She said she had already verified the facts of the situation before bringing it to my attention. She was convinced it was true. I wasn't surprised by the information TW shared with me. Deep down inside, I knew it was true, too. I had suspected for months that Dave was seeing other women again, and that was why I had asked him to move out. But no one in our office was aware of the separation—I thought I could keep it to myself. Now, apparently, everyone was aware of it.

NOW I HAD TO FACE THE FACT THAT EVERYONE I WORKED WITH WAS AWARE OF MY PERSONAL PREDICAMENT.

I was shocked that not one of the male colleagues, with whom I worked closely, came to me first. When I went to them with TW's information, they all confirmed it, but none of them had come to me on their own. I was disappointed with them. Nonetheless, TW's bravery impressed me. It took a lot of courage on her part to approach me with something like this. She was willing to speak the truth to me. I have held her in high esteem ever since. In that same conversation I told TW about the separation and thanked her for her honesty. She left knowing she had done the right thing.

Now I had to face the fact that everyone I worked with was aware of my personal predicament. I had been living with the hope of reconciliation and restoration in my marriage for four years, but it seemed more and more obvious that I was just unwilling to accept that the marriage had fallen apart a long time ago. At the beginning, Dave and I had gone to marriage counseling, but it ended abruptly when the counselor informed Dave that it was a waste of money to continue with the therapy until he decided whether or not he wanted to be married. Four years later he still hadn't decided.

If my friends and coworkers knew about my husband's continual infidelity, they had to be wondering why I was putting up with this type of behavior in my marriage. I had to wonder myself. I decided at that moment that it was time for a divorce.

At first I wasn't sure what to do or where to start. I remembered that I had attended several fundraising banquets for The Women's Resource Center of Sarasota County — a place for women who needed help. I called and set an appointment to talk with a counselor. Sitting there, I had a good cry. I was given some wise counsel about how to find a reputable attorney and what steps I needed to take next in order to file for divorce. My marriage would be dissolved within three months.

Tin Woman and Scarecrow were already workmates and friends. As I opened up and allowed TW into my inner circle, she, too, became someone I found I could rely on for help. We truly were opposites, but that made our friendship all the more interesting. What I wasn't good at, she excelled at! I found her to be a very astute business woman with a knack for building good relationships with everyone at work, even those who moved on to other career endeavors.

She was very kind hearted, and everyone knew it! TW was married, so I tried not to impose too much or interrupt her family time — not that she would have minded. A few years later, when she went through her own divorce, we drew even closer together.

There was no tap dancing from this Tin Woman, and no tooting cap, but she did enjoy a good party on occasion. Over a glass of wine, we would have some terrific girl-to-girl talks.

L. Frank Baum's Tin Man was quite a daredevil, always ready to fight on behalf of the weak and downtrodden. TW didn't carry an axe, but she was a strong woman. You'll hear later how my Tin Woman came to the rescue and protected me when I was helpless to protect myself!

Chapter 11 | THE LION

Dorothy, the Scarecrow, and the Tin Man paused, clutched each other's hands, and slowly moved forward into the dark forest. In their fear, they exclaimed, "Lions and tigers and bears, oh my!" over and over again. Each time their voices grew louder, and the chant got faster. A sudden, terrifying growl introduced them to the Cowardly Lion.

In the movie version, I think what makes the Lion so loveable is that he's such an artist! I'm not sure which scene I appreciate more. There's the initial meeting in which he bullies out phrases like "Put 'em up! Put 'em up! Trying to sneak up on me, eh? Trying to pull an axe on me, eh?"—only to cry like baby when Dorothy rebukes him. Then there's the amazing soliloquy outside the Wizard's meeting room, where the Lion boldly imagines the possibilities, "if I were King of the forrrestttt."

It seems that the King of Beasts was a bit of a drama queen, to say the least—and we love him all the more for it. My Lion is an artist too, but without the theatrical temperament. He's a jazz pianist, and a very accomplished one at that! So often, just listening to his music soothed my tormented spirit.

Trying to enjoy myself a little on my journey through Oz, I agreed to meet a good friend at an outdoor restaurant called Mattison's City Grille. Every Sunday she gathered there with other jazz enthusiasts to hear the sounds of Debbie Keeton and her ensemble, Eclectic. I usually didn't venture out much in the evenings for entertainment, but I found this place to be a safe haven where I could kick back and enjoy some delightful music and conversation with these fellow jazz lovers.

The Lion was the pianist in this well-loved group. Aside from being very talented, he was always very kind and polite to me. Often he would come by and chat during intermission. The Lion had gone through a divorce himself and recently lost his mother. I had just lost my dad. It seemed we were the only two people there under the age of fifty-five, and we became friends. One day, the Lion asked me out on a date and I accepted. It was a perfect date and we connected in a wonderful way. It was so perfect that I got scared. By this time, I was taking a number of prescribed medications. With that in mind, I knew that I needed to be very careful with dating relationships. I told the Lion that I couldn't get involved. He decided to stick around anyway. He became my third traveling companion.

Dorothy's Lion transformed over time from a fearful coward to the King of Beasts. My Lion, however, was a hero from the start. Although his music was gentle and soothing, he himself was tall and strong. He often told me that he felt "commissioned" to watch over me. Quite frankly, I needed that. Between the crazy mood swings of my medicated state and my naïve understanding of the world, I was sometimes a sitting duck. I am thankful not only for the close friendship that developed between us, but for the fact that God had sent me a bodyguard.

WHEN YOU FEEL ALONE IN THE WORLD AND AFRAID, IT IS A WONDERFUL THING TO HAVE SOMEONE WHO CHECKS UP ON YOU TO MAKE SURE YOU'RE WELL.

For three years, the Lion was one of my closest companions. His loud roar was one of encouragement — encouragement that powerfully impacted my ability to heal. In his own loving way, he nurtured me. Through his hugs and his listening ear, God brought restoration to my soul. I have never met such a kind-hearted person as the Lion. One of the things he did was to call me every day. When you feel alone in the world and afraid, it is a wonderful thing to have someone who checks up on you to make sure you're well. We did a lot of things together. We saw movies, went to concerts, read books, and had many interesting conversations.

The Lion is very intelligent. I always enjoyed his insights and his company. He was the strength behind my moving forward in writing this book and taking action to do what I was destined to do in life.

When I left Oz, I said goodbye and left the Lion behind. I hated that because I knew he so desperately wanted to stay by my side, to love me, and protect me. I was very saddened in knowing that I was inflicting pain upon his heart, when he had never been anything but wonderful to me. Yet back in Kansas, I knew I had a mission to accomplish—one that would require all my energy and focus. I knew I would not be able to give the Lion the love and attention he deserved.

So regretfully I continued on my journey alone, believing that God would care for the Lion in a way that would far surpass anything I was capable of doing. I will always hold a special place for him in my heart.

Chapter 12

THE FIELD OF POPPIES

The Wicked Witch cringes as she looks through her crystal ball and sees that Dorothy and her companions are getting closer to the Emerald City. She so desperately wants to kill Dorothy and take the ruby slippers for herself. In the movie, the Witch mixes up a potion and moves toward her crystal ball, a flying monkey by her side. "Something with poison in it," she mutters, "but attractive to the eye and soothing to smell. Poppies... Poppies... Poppies will put them to sleep."

As the friends make their way out of the Dark Forest, they realize that the Emerald City is now in view. Straight ahead, their hopes for "a brain, a heart, a home, and the nerve" await them. All they have to do is cross the meadow filled with red poppies.

It's such an incredibly beautiful field of flowers, yet the travelers barely notice, because their eyes are focused on their ultimate destination, the spectacular Emerald City.

"Let's go!" says the Scarecrow enthusiastically.

"Yes, let's run!" Dorothy responds.

Unaware of the danger, they set off with excitement, almost making it to the other side before stopping to lie down and rest... perhaps forever.

In the book it happens a little differently. The Scarecrow takes note of the poppies immediately, and warns everyone that if they don't get through the field quickly, Dorothy, Toto and the Lion will die from the scent of the opium. He instructs the Lion to run as fast as he can, because he is much too heavy for anyone to carry him. Not being human, the Scarecrow and the Tin Man are immune to the poisonous smell. They make a chair with their arms and carry Dorothy and Toto to safety.

I find a lot of life lessons in this great piece of literature. There are several truths worth noting here. First, it is not uncommon to find an enormous obstacle in our way, just when our goal is in view. Second, whether you call it the Witch, the Devil, the Dark Side of the Force, or just plain old Evil, I do believe there is a strong, negative power out to possess us, strip us of our most precious gifts, and leave us for dead, so that we can never reach our full potential or accomplish the purposes we were created for. Third, there are fields of poppies all around us, and we are all susceptible. These are places that look good and promise to make you feel great, but if you stay too long, you'll die there. Alcohol, drugs, sexual promiscuity and pornography are but a few.

How many people, after a difficult time or a traumatic experience, find themselves drinking away their sorrows or getting high to ease the pain? Maybe going from one sexual relationship to another provides some sense of security. Or fantasizing gives the illusion that ones dreams are more exciting than reality. Regardless of the field we choose, the pleasure and relief is only temporary. What starts off as a little something to soothe our nerves or push away the pain for awhile can become a bondage we're held in for a long time… maybe even permanently.

WHAT STARTS OFF AS A LITTLE SOMETHING TO SOOTHE OUR NERVES OR PUSH AWAY THE PAIN FOR AWHILE CAN BECOME A BONDAGE WE'RE HELD IN FOR A LONG TIME… MAYBE EVEN PERMANENTLY.

These poppy fields don't only consist of dark, immoral or illegal behaviors. Obsessive work, exercise, shopping or socializing—even becoming a recluse in one's own home—really anything that prevents us from moving forward and living our lives to the fullest, can ultimately enslave us. The struggle, and a struggle it is, is to get through the field and move forward in life. I found myself in a Field of Poppies when I was over-medicated with prescription drugs by my doctor.

When I first arrived in Florida, I remember driving over the Skyway Bridge for the first time with my mother. I was a bit intimidated by its size and height. As we drove up to the top and down the other side, I found I couldn't listen to my mother talking. I was too busy praying quietly as I drove. Later, we laughed about how it was a little scary getting across that bridge.

Not long afterward, I learned that my husband had been unfaithful to me on multiple occasions. It hit me hard and unexpectedly, but I was a strong woman and I thought I could handle it. I underestimated the amount of stress that it would cause me physically, emotionally, and spiritually.

Sometimes you can talk your way through a stressful situation and take control of your thoughts. Sometimes you can manage your stress with deep breathing and other calming techniques and strategies. But when the stress is very high—when you're bombarded from all different sides with multiple stressful situations—the effects can be debilitating.

I started to notice that I became very uncomfortable whenever I had to go over that Skyway Bridge. That, in itself, unnerved me! I would blast the radio and sing along as loudly as I could to keep myself from thinking how frightened I was. Or I would try to talk myself over the bridge with slow, methodical breathing and words of affirmation like "You're doing just fine!" and "That's it! Keep going! You're almost there!" Eventually I just began avoiding the bridge altogether, so that I wouldn't put myself in that extremely, uncomfortable dilemma.

Occasionally, there was no way around it: the bridge had to be crossed. One morning, as I started across, breathing slowly and calmly, talking myself through the process, something very unusual happened. I felt as if my head was detaching from my body. Like a balloon, it seemed to be floating away.

"No!" I thought. "Not now! I need my head to stay with me for this! Don't leave me! Come back!" I shouted from the driver's seat. "Come back!"

I quickly turned up the radio, only to find my mind further confused and distracted. The words and music seemed to scramble themselves in my brain. They seemed trapped, unable to move through my mind. I shut it off immediately. Panic struck, I tried every relaxation technique I knew of, one after another, until I reached the other side. Somehow, I made it over the bridge that day, but it was a terrifying experience. Had my newly divorced status, along with crossing this monster of a bridge heightened my stress level beyond my limits? Apparently so.

I continued to avoid the bridge at all costs, but ultimately stress reared its ugly head again. The next time I had such a frightening experience, I was driving my car on an ordinary two-lane street.

"What's going on?" I thought. I wasn't on the Skyway. I was just in the local neighborhood. I didn't know that I was having panic attacks. I didn't know what a panic attack was. What I did know was that I was out of control. I needed help. I decided to talk to my doctor and get some expert advice on the matter.

The only doctor I had at the time was my gynecologist. We had a good relationship, so I felt comfortable explaining to her what I was experiencing. At first, her advice was the same I'd heard from friends:

"You've been through a difficult time. You need to relax. Have a glass of wine at night to take the edge off."

I didn't really like that answer. At the time, I hadn't had any alcohol in twenty years. Her next suggestion was to try medication; she prescribed an anti-depressant. I grew concerned as I read through the literature on the drug—all the potential side effects and complications. I had been opposed to taking any unnecessary drugs or medications, from the moment I became a mother. I didn't even like to take aspirin. But desperate to alleviate the anxiety attacks, I decided to give it a try. After the first dose, I was struck with the worse migraine of my life. So I decided to try that glass of wine.

I GREW CONCERNED AS I READ THROUGH THE LITERATURE ON THE DRUG — ALL THE POTENTIAL SIDE EFFECTS AND COMPLICATIONS.

Unfortunately, the panic attacks continued, so my doctor prescribed Xanex. I was encouraged to take a small dose of the medication any time I felt myself getting over-anxious. I followed the instructions, and for a short time it seemed to work. Then the attacks returned and grew more frequent. Not knowing what to do, I called my doctor in the middle of an attack and left a frantic message asking if I should increase the dose of the medication.

"Should I start taking it two or three times a day?" I asked hysterically. I desperately waited for a return phone call. The assistant who checked the doctor's voice mail called me back with a discouraging reply:

"Gail, we received your message, and the doctor would like you to see a psychiatrist. We'll give you a list of local doctors from which you can choose one."

"A psychiatrist?" I thought to myself, "A psychiatrist? Oh my God! I can't go to a psychiatrist! My father would never approve of such a thing!"

I had been brought up with an old school perspective. My folks emphasized the importance of privacy. Today the idea of going to therapy is widely accepted and even routine for many people. In my parents' day, it was viewed much differently. Needing to see a psychiatrist meant that you were insane — literally. Crazy people ended up in institutions. Weak people talked to doctors to help them with their problems. Strong people resolved their issues on their own.

This was not good. What was I to do? I had actually been going to see a counselor for several months, but going to a psychiatrist seemed like a much more serious, even drastic step. I put the phone down, my head dropped, and I cried in embarrassment.

The next time I went to see the counselor, we talked about the doctor's recommendation and my concerns. The counselor explained that the psychiatrist's role was to do an initial evaluation, prescribe medication, monitor my response to it, and make any necessary changes. The goal was to get the right type of medication and the exact dosage that would alleviate the intense anxiety I was experiencing. At the same time, I would continue to work through my issues with my regular counselor. After we had resolved my emotional issues one by one, I would be weaned off of the medication with the psychiatrist's help. That didn't sound so bad. In fact, it made a good deal of sense. And it wasn't like I had a whole lot of choice here, anyway… my head was floating away. I was suffering from a mild depression resulting from the divorce and all it entailed, and I couldn't control the frequent panic attacks on my own. I agreed to see the psychiatrist, follow her guidance regarding the medication, and continue with counseling in pursuit of wholeness and healing.

Eventually, I came to think of my counselor like Dorothy's Wizard—someone who could help me find my way home to Sanity. I loved this Wizard! We met regularly, and our talks were truly beneficial to me. The meetings with the psychiatrist were not so beneficial. It wasn't as much the psychiatrist herself, as the process of finding the right medication that would work for me. The whole procedure made me feel like a guinea pig. The doctor would choose a medicine, and I would have to start taking it gradually over a period of weeks. Reporting for regular visits, I would describe how I was feeling and mention any side effects I was experiencing.

One time, I was in the movie theater with a friend, and I was sure I saw a very large scorpion crawling up the center aisle. Intellectually I knew that there could not be a giant scorpion in the theater, yet my eyes still saw one. I even lifted up my feet as it passed. My friend and I chuckled about it afterwards. But these kind of side effects were fairly typical. Whenever I told the doctor about them, she changed either the dose or the medication itself. If she decided to change the medication, I had to be slowly weaned off of the old one and then start over (gradually again) with something new.

When we found the right medication and dosage for me, the results were wonderful. My spirit was lifted—I had significantly less anxiety. Then just as I began to enjoy the facade of normalcy, I'd start having side effects or it would stop working for me and we'd have to start over with another new medication. It was brutal! Sometimes, I was heavily medicated. Other times I had headaches. Occasionally there were hallucinations. In between different medications, I'd go back to drinking those glasses of wine, hoping for some relief. Very often I felt scatter-brained. Mentally, things were blurry and out of focus. The wine didn't get me intoxicated, but it did seem to help me let go of the confusion in my head, so that I could think more calmly and clearly.

Let me take a moment here to say that although I found this guinea pig method of prescribing the right doses and medications to patients to be less than admirable, that's the way it's done. The medication, overall, helped me get through a very difficult time. This endeavor should always be done under the watchful eye of a specialized physician.

For me, the medication went on for months, which turned into years. I spent much more time in this place than I had hoped or imagined. My counselor had talked to me at length about the possibility of being on prescribed medication indefinitely. Sometimes that's necessary. I didn't like the drugs, but I'd gotten used to them. In fact, I'd grown dependent on them. I was convinced that without the medication, the anxiety attacks would return and I'd completely fall apart. Family and friends were beginning to express concern. I was just not myself. The Lion told me that he knew I had some specific goals in life, and that he thought the side effects of the medication could be a significant deterrent to my success. My youngest daughter Grace, who lived with me at the time, hated the medication. She saw all the complications I experienced day in and day out, and from one month to the next. Though I didn't know it, she had begun praying that God would deliver me from what she saw as a bondage. One day, she announced:

I DIDN'T LIKE THE DRUGS, BUT I'D GOTTEN USED TO THEM. IN FACT, I'D GROWN DEPENDENT ON THEM.

"Mom, I think you need to get off that medicine now. I've been praying for you and I think you've been healed!"

I thought this was a sweet gesture on my daughter's part, and I do believe in the power of prayer. But I was looking at this situation strictly from a practical perspective. My spiritual insight seemed to have diminished during my use of prescription drugs. The medications had numbed me, which kept me from feeling extreme pain and fear. But I was also no longer as sensitive to the presence of God, not as aware of His perspective on the circumstances of my life.

I had been seeing the psychiatrist for about two years, and I'd had a good stretch where—in conjunction with a glass of wine or two each evening—the medication seemed to be working effectively. But strange side effects would once more disrupt everything. I started hallucinating again. I remember going to lunch with some friends, and when I went into the restroom, I saw a large black lab quietly sitting in the corner, panting. I knew it wasn't real—the dog wasn't really there—but still, I saw him.

I rarely drove my car anymore—partly because I was drinking in the evenings, and I didn't want to drink and drive. But there was more to it than that. I had become slightly paranoid and didn't want the responsibility of driving, because I couldn't be sure what hallucinations or other physical symptoms I might encounter. My psychiatrist began to give me additional medication to counteract the side effects of the current medication. Then all my medications were changed and a new one was added. The doctor urged me to give the new drug a chance. It would take time to work up to the full (most effective) dosage. I was told not to be concerned if I initially experienced some minor side effects.

I went away on vacation to visit my sister. This new medication was so strong, I couldn't do much of anything. I tried to be optimistic and see it as a much-needed rest. By the time I returned home, I noticed that when I wasn't continually falling asleep, I was constantly crying. Frustration and despair began to set in.

Arriving at work one morning, I was hesitant to go inside the office building, realizing that I had sunk to one of the lowest places I'd ever been in life. It wasn't that I was suicidal. I'd had those kinds of thoughts only briefly, immediately following the divorce. I had determined then that I wouldn't go that route for the sake of my children. That's when I first sought professional counseling. This time the despair was different. It came with the realization that I could be medicated for the rest of my life, and that if so, I would never be able to fulfill God's purpose for me — not in this condition. I lowered my head, disappointed in where life had brought me.

"God, please help me," I whispered. As tears streamed down my face and onto my lap, God spoke to my heart firmly, insistently:

"Don't you give up on Me, Gail! Don't you give up!"

Those words sounded familiar… Where had I heard them before? They were the same words I had cried out to my son. Joe, when he had been unconscious and nearly died. God continued to speak to me:

"You are so close to the end of this valley. All the gifts, visions, dreams, and ministry that I've told you about are right around the corner. Don't give up! You need to understand that I've only shown you the tip of the iceberg. There is so much more that awaits you! Look at how much Joe's life has changed in a year. By this time next year, you'll barely recognize your life. It will be so different. Don't give up, Gail!"

I COULD FEEL THE PRESENCE OF GOD'S SPIRIT SO STRONGLY AS I SAT THERE IN THE CAR. I KNEW I HAD HEARD HIS VOICE.

I could feel the presence of God's Spirit so strongly as I sat there in the car. I knew I had heard His voice. Confidently I emerged from my car, and walked to my office, knowing what I had to do. I wasted no time in picking up the phone and calling the psychiatrist. I set an appointment to meet with her at her earliest opportunity.

A few days later, I found myself sitting in the doctor's office in tears (thanks to the newest medication). I asked her to take me off the drugs immediately. She had reservations, watching me weep uncontrollably, something she had never seen me do before. I told her that I was sure I was overmedicated, and that I wanted to get off of everything right away.

"Look at me," I cried. "I'm never like this! I can't even carry on a conversation with you, or anyone else, without bursting into tears. It's this medication." I paused and took in a long, deep breath and continued. "I think I'm actually okay underneath all this. I've been faithful with my counseling all this time. I've worked out my issues. I know it's time to get off all this medicine!" Then I offered a proposition: "If I get off, and I can't handle things, I can always go back on. But I want off, and I want off now!"

She wasn't convinced. She started talking about getting a brain scan, testing for this and that.

"There's nothing wrong with my brain!" I insisted. "I just need to get off this medicine!" Seeing my determination, she agreed to create a schedule to wean me off each of the medications.

"And what about this one?" I asked, as I held up the newest prescription bottle.

"What's that?" she responded.

"It's the other medication you prescribed."

"I never prescribed that to you," she said.

"Yes, you did!"

It turned out that the last time she had changed my medications, what she determined to prescribe, and what she actually called in to the pharmacy were two different things. I later checked with the pharmacy and confirmed that the mistake was hers. There are many anti-depressants that all attempt to do the same thing — they work in similar ways to achieve similar results. But how a person reacts to each of those drugs can be extremely different. This doctor had called in a drug that was much like that which I was accustomed to taking, but for me, this particular drug had horrific side effects. The fact was she thought she had prescribed something else.

Feeling that I was finally on my way to freedom, I chose to disregard her error. The doctor gave me a schedule to follow and I would soon begin weaning off the drugs. When I got home, however, I realized her plan was so gradual—so long and drawn out—that I would have to go to the pharmacy and buy more of these terrible medications in order to follow her exact exit plan. It would take months. I didn't want to do that. I was determined to develop my own plan, carefully keeping in mind the importance of weaning off the medications gradually. It may not have been the wisest move on my part, but I laid all the pills out on my bed, and set up my own consolidated schedule, which didn't require a new purchase, and didn't take quite so long.

Looking back, I should have worked more closely with the psychiatrist on a weaning off plan that was more suitable for me. I would never again make the decision to determine that procedure myself. I am not a specialist in pharmaceuticals and their effects on people. My plan could have had dangerous repercussions. I am also not saying that everyone is destined to be totally drug-free. In my specific situation, I truly felt a healing had taken place underneath all the medicine, and I elected to take steps to see if that was the case. I do believe that continued medication may be appropriate for some. That decision should be made wisely between each individual and his or her doctor.

Every morning I got up with confidence, determined to stick to my plan. It wasn't easy. At times it truly was a battle of the mind. Everyday, I drew close to God in prayer asking Him for help. As conflicts arose at work or at home, I would hear a voice in the back of my mind saying, "You're getting upset, better take the medicine! That's what the doctor prescribed that medicine for. You should take it! You need it! It's just that one pill. Go on, take it!"

In frustration, I would shout out loud, "I am not taking any more medication!" I had to fight for my freedom, and with God's help, I won! I re-taught myself to deal with each conflict that arose, on an incident-by-incident basis. I reminded myself to breathe slowly, and think things through.

LOOKING BACK AT WHAT I WENT THROUGH OVER A FOUR-YEAR PERIOD, IT'S NO WONDER THAT I HAD STARTED HAVING THOSE PANIC ATTACKS.

Before I knew it, I was drug-free! I had my life back. I could think again. I could read again. It was like a re-birth. I realized that beneath all the symptoms and side effects of the medication, a genuine healing had taken place. I had originally started the medication to help alleviate my depression and control my anxiety, while I went to counseling to work on my issues. All that counseling had been successful! I no longer had ten or fifteen major issues to deal with. My burden had been reduced to one or two small problems at any given time.

Looking back at what I went through over a four-year period, it's no wonder that I had started having those panic attacks. One after another, and sometimes simultaneously, I faced the following:

» My husband's rejection of me, his betrayal, and infidelity

» The death of my twenty-year marriage

» Broken trust, loss of confidence and self-esteem

» The death of many lifelong dreams

» Significant (bordering on unhealthy) weight loss

» Withdrawal from friends and family, the desire to avoid social situations

» Life as a single woman, head of household, single parent of three teenagers

» Feelings of frustration in not being able to fix things for my children

» Feelings of failure in not being there emotionally for my children

» Being the sole provider for my family

» Having full responsibility for children's college costs

» My father's illness and death

» My mother's battle with breast cancer

» My daughter's struggles with college

» Having my son crash the car while drinking and driving

- » Seeing my son almost die of a drug overdose

- » Watching my son go to jail

- » Experiencing sexual discrimination in the workplace

- » Experiencing sexual intimidation by a business associate

- » Being rejected (because of my divorce) by Christian ministers and friends

- » Managing my own use of alcohol and prescription drugs

- » Numerous health problems (including a cancer scare) resulting in countless doctor's visits, tests, and medications

Sometimes it's just too much!

Three months after I'd gone off my medications, I got a call from the psychiatrist checking in to see how I was making out. She was astonished when I told her that I was drug-free and doing well. She asked me how I was coping with things. I told her I was making it through life just fine by taking one day at time, and relying on prayer.

What astonished me was the praise that I received from all my other doctors. My general doctor, my gynecologist, my neurologist, my physical therapist, and even my dentist were all ecstatic that I had found freedom and deliverance from the psychiatrist's medicine cabinet. Nearly every one of them said they had seen patients who got stuck there forever.

Thanks to Glinda the Good, Dorothy, Toto and the Lion awoke from their drug-induced sleep, joyfully regrouped with their friends the Scarecrow and the Tin Man, and moved forward, arm in arm, toward the Emerald City.

As for me, I know God had heard the prayers of my daughter and my Lion, as well as many others. He heard the groaning of my heart as my dreams nearly slipped away into a coma forever. He used the Wizard to bring healing to my mind. But the glory belongs to Him. Without His love and protection, without His miraculous power, I might still be in the Field of Poppies.

"And if the Son sets you free, you will be free indeed!" (John 8:36)

Chapter 13 | THE GREEN GLASSES

In the original story of *The Wonderful Wizard of Oz*, Dorothy and her friends finally arrive at the Emerald City and are greeted by the Guardian of the Gates. They are each perfectly fitted with a pair of green glasses, which are locked securely upon their heads—so securely that the glasses can't be removed. This ensures that this magnificent city appears as colorful as the Wizard intends for it to. Walking down the streets, with her new head gear comfortably in place, Dorothy is amazed to find that everything in the Emerald City is, in fact, some beautiful shade of green. When she and her friends leave the city, the Guardian of the Gates removes their glasses and their vision returns to normal.

From the onset of my journey, I felt as if I, too, had somehow been fitted with a most interesting pair of spectacles that colored my perspective on everything. These spectacles were tinted with the muted hues that can only come from that of a rejected heart. When I was healthy, happy, and whole, I saw myself as a strong, confident woman who could do just about anything she wanted to. My outlook on life was clear and optimistic. After my divorce, everything seemed dark, dismal and ill-defined. My surroundings were greatly deprived of energy, joy, and opportunity, and seemed to have an unfortunate overabundance of negativity. The only thing colorful was the language. I found the whole thing a difficult sight to take in! Unfortunately, these glasses were secured in place for almost the entire duration of my trip. It grieved me to see things the way I did. The unpleasantness of the world forced me to retreat within myself.

I would love to report that the multiple affairs of my husband had no effect on me, but in reality, the opposite was true. Each one of his indiscretions tore away at my heart, layer by layer, until nothing remained. When the divorce was complete, I was transformed into a victim of rejection. I quickly took note that this had produced in me an insatiable desire for love and acceptance which made me extremely vulnerable. Fortunately, I came to this realization early in my journey, and took measures to protect myself.

WHEN THE DIVORCE WAS COMPLETE, I WAS TRANSFORMED INTO A VICTIM OF REJECTION. I QUICKLY TOOK NOTE THAT THIS HAD PRODUCED IN ME AN INSATIABLE DESIRE FOR LOVE AND ACCEPTANCE WHICH MADE ME EXTREMELY VULNERABLE.

Stepping out into the world as a single woman, after twenty years of marriage, I knew I needed to be mindful that there were men out there who might try to take advantage of my vulnerability. As I mentioned earlier, I knew it was important for me to focus my time and energy on my personal healing, and I had decided not to pursue dating relationships. Quite frankly, I was scared to death of the whole nightclub, dating atmosphere and was quite content to avoid it. The thought of getting myself into a situation that might compromise my Christian values frightened me. I had enough problems without adding something like that to my list. In my vulnerable state, I knew I was a prime candidate for what I refer to as the "revolving door of relationships" or "looking for love in all the wrong places." It's one of the most common pitfalls for wounded women, and that's why I bring it up.

For the most part, I did manage to avoid this pitfall, though I was tested once and didn't fare so well. About two years after the divorce, out of the blue, a business acquaintance mentioned that he had been admiring me from afar. I was surprised. I didn't think this person even liked me. I stressed how important I thought it was for people to really get to know each other before dating. When he responded positively to that, I thought that was a good sign. I so desperately wanted to have a friend. This man went out of his way to bump into me, write notes, send texts and call me by phone just to chat. At first I didn't take it seriously. I thought it was kind of funny, but he was serious about pursuing me. His persistence caught me off guard and I found that I felt rather flattered. A few times, he asked me to meet him so that we could talk, and I did. They were brief encounters, kind of mysterious and intriguing. It's funny how dating games never change. You can be sixteen or forty-six… It always feels good to have someone pay attention to you. Within two weeks, however, I was in over my head.

In our flirtatious exchanges, I found myself saying things that really pushed the limits of my Christian boundaries — things I didn't really mean. I was caught up in the game. But it all ended abruptly… the man was involved in another relationship. This was just a game that wasn't meant to go anywhere. I wasn't a skilled game player and I'm not sure he was either. But regardless, the game we were playing was over.

What was I thinking? That's just it, I *wasn't* thinking! I felt like such a fool. I had to take responsibility for how I had behaved, how I had portrayed myself, how I had participated in the flirtation. In my vulnerability, I was sending all kinds of signals. I was fortunate that things stopped when they did. I determined to be more careful in the future. I didn't want to go through that again and again and again until I found the right guy. The revolving door of relationships was definitely not for me.

Of course, it's so easy to say all that. Our hearts so desperately want to be loved. That's what makes it so difficult. That's why the door is a revolving door. It moves around and around so easily. The reality was that my heart still needed healing and my vision was still skewed. I was lucky to have been thrown from the doorway!

For a while, my feelings were hurt, but eventually I got over it. At the time, I think the guy felt bad about it himself. But what happened next was totally unexpected. Over the next year and a half, I would often find myself in the same business circles as this individual. Sometimes it was fine. But other times, he would start playing the game again, flirting with me and making suggestive comments. I became extremely uncomfortable around him, to the point of feeling threatened. It was as if he had this strange power over me. I could feel myself cowering inside, and I didn't like that.

I had thought I made it clear that I just wanted to be friends. I tried to stand up for myself, but I didn't want to hurt his feelings. I thought we could just be friends, go back to a polite but professional relationship. Apparently not. At one point, he cornered me in a stairwell. Somehow I quickly managed to slip away. His actions were never overt enough or aggressive enough to the point of physical harm. But they were intimidating and emotionally inappropriate.

If this had happened before my divorce, when I was spectacle-free, I wouldn't have thought twice about boldly putting this man in his place. But during this time, it didn't happen that way. I felt confused, weak and helpless. I decided to confide in TW, my Tin Woman — after all, that's what girlfriends are for. They support you when you can't support yourself.

At first, I was embarrassed to tell her the story. What would she think of me? I was a Christian woman. I was supposed to have it all together. I wasn't supposed to get caught up in a foolish flirtation like that. But I was even more embarrassed and afraid of what might happen if I didn't tell someone what was going on. I needed help. So I put my pride aside and laid out the whole story.

The only other person who knew about it was my Scarecrow, SK. I had told him from the very start and sworn him to secrecy. When I came back later to tell him the direction that things had taken, he pointed out my victimized posture. SK suggested that TW, being a woman, was in a better position to help me in this particular situation. We agreed that a confrontation was necessary, and that in this case, TW would probably be the most effective.

I've always believed that secrets can be used to overpower and intimidate, even manipulate people. But when those secrets are exposed, that power is dissolved.

TW already knew the individual. When she found out he was harassing me, she went straight to him and confronted him on my behalf. He backed off immediately. It was a long time before he came near me again. By the time he did, I had gained significant strength on my road to recovery, and I was able to stand up for myself.

Fortunately, those awful glasses that colored my world with rejection would fall off by the time my journey was complete. Eventually they would be permanently replaced by the regular "readers" that all of us over forty wear, so that we can read what's put in front of us. Now those are glasses I can live with!

Chapter 14 | THE EMERALD CITY

When Dorothy and her friends arrived inside the gates of the Emerald City, they were awestruck. The city was hustling and bustling with all sorts of people and activity. I remember watching the movie, absolutely amazed by the horse that continually changed colors as it as pulled Dorothy's carriage.

It was several days before Dorothy, the Scarecrow, the Tin Man, and the Lion were actually allowed to see the Wizard. While they waited, they were treated to the best of the Emerald City's hospitality—fed the most delicious foods, given the softest beds on which to rest and recover from their journey. They were also pampered, primped and polished so that they would look their very best. Only then would they be presented before the great Wizard of Oz.

There is nothing that feels better after a long journey than some rest and relaxation at the local spa. Before I came to Oz, my life had only a taste of such things. Our finances didn't allow much "extravagance." When I returned to the corporate world, I understood it was important to look the part of a successful, professional businesswoman. It's just part of the job. So I kept regular appointments at both the hair and the nail salons. I noticed right away that it made me feel better about myself. I do believe that feeling good about our appearance gives us an added air of confidence. We walk a little taller and our smile is a little brighter.

I DO BELIEVE THAT FEELING GOOD ABOUT OUR APPEARANCE GIVES US AN ADDED AIR OF CONFIDENCE. WE WALK A LITTLE TALLER AND OUR SMILE IS A LITTLE BRIGHTER.

Living in Florida does have its advantages! It daily offered me several picturesque beaches within a fifteen-minute drive. A stroll by the shore a few evenings a week is always calming and cost-free!

As my marriage began to crumble, however, I found that it took a toll on me physically. It's unbelievable how tight and twisted your body can become in response to emotional stress. After the divorce, the stress only increased. Fear of living alone, worrying about making enough money to pay the bills, concern over my children's welfare, and dealing with my own state of mind continued to weigh heavily upon me. My system was overloaded.

An exercise program at the local YMCA significantly helped in lowering the stress level and keeping me healthy. At different stages, I was more consistent than at others. (Both depression and medication brought exercise to a standstill.) I also found that regular chiropractic adjustments and massages were necessary to give me at least some temporary relief from the physical pain I was experiencing.

Another place I found relaxation was the local tanning salon. Yes, I lived minutes from one of the most beautiful beaches in the world, but I rarely had time to bask in the sun for hours. A weekly fifteen-minute visit to the salon helped me to relax and gave me a healthy glow. I also decided to get my teeth whitened. It was a fairly inexpensive procedure and made my smile, (even if it wasn't genuine), look beautiful. My teenage girls also helped me with fashion makeovers and facials. They wanted to do all they could to help their mom look and feel her best!

Then, a few months before my divorce became final, I started thinking about cosmetic surgery. My husband had said some really negative things about my physical appearance that wounded me deeply. Somehow I couldn't let those words go. I might as well be frank: he complained that my breasts were droopy and my butt was flat. I took a long hard look in the mirror. I had always thought my body looked just fine, but standing there naked, I had to admit there was some truth to what he'd said. I might have laughed it off, if I hadn't realized that he was comparing me unfavorably to other women he had slept with. The rejection was unbearable. It made me feel unbelievably insecure and unattractive.

I used to think it was crazy to even consider cosmetic surgery — we should all be satisfied with the bodies we've been given. But when I realized that I was in a place financially where I could afford to make some changes, I decided I would. I didn't want to please my husband; our marriage was already over. I just wanted to pull myself together and put things back where they belonged. I felt it would give me a fresh start as a single woman.

We really live in an amazing era. If you have the money, you can refresh and restore your body in many ways. I started researching breast enlargement and augmentation — not that I particularly needed a larger set of breasts, but I wanted mine lifted. And since my hips tended to be larger, larger breasts would give me a better proportioned body. After a consultation and several months of consideration, I went through with the surgery and it was a great success. I have never regretted that decision.

I must confess that my indulgence in cosmetic surgery was not limited to breast enlargement and augmentation. Since I was a child, I had been teased about the size of my nose. Everybody at one time or another had made a comment about it. One night I was driving home from an event downtown, and a drunk guy in a taxi yelled to me, "Hey beautiful!" I glanced quickly in his direction and then turned away. He responded by yelling out, "Your nose is too big anyway!" I know, I know. Who cares what a drunken stranger in a taxi thinks about your appearance? But it was the straw that broke the camel's back. I decided to get a nose job.

Even so, I didn't want to turn myself into a clone of someone I wasn't. I sat in a room full of women one evening at a networking event. I was amazed to find several "Barbie dolls." They all looked beautiful, but they all looked the same. Long, straight blonde hair, tight faces, tight bodies, all perfectly shaped, and all identical. As I scanned the room, I began to appreciate the unique looks of others who had chosen not to take that route. Colorful hair, bodies of various sizes and shapes, chins and noses that had a family history behind them. They were unique and they looked good!

Fortunately, I had a great doctor. With my breast surgery, I had begged him, "Please don't let me come out of this looking like Dolly Parton!" I knew that would not be a good reflection of who I was. He assured me he would do his best to give me breasts that fit my size, and he did. With this second surgery, he assured me that my nose would still look like mine, only a little straighter and a little smaller, and it did. In both cases, other than the members of my immediate family, no one really noticed the transformation or attributed it to surgery. People thought that I was looking good. They just couldn't quite put their finger on what was different about me.

I will say that there is one great pitfall in making significant changes to your physical appearance. I found this out for myself, and I've chosen to discuss it here, because I know that many women experience this. Between the nails and the hair, the white teeth, the tanned body, the weight loss (accented by a brand new wardrobe), and then on top of it all, the cosmetic surgery, I must say, I looked great! On the outside, it was amazing. But on the inside, I felt totally empty — a shell of a woman. I liked looking beautiful; I hoped it would distract people and keep them from seeing my brokenness. I felt like "Gail"—the woman I thought I was, the woman I had always been — had died during the divorce. My spirit, my personality, my zest for life…they were all gone.

ON THE OUTSIDE, IT WAS AMAZING. BUT ON THE INSIDE, I FELT TOTALLY EMPTY — A SHELL OF A WOMAN.

Unfortunately, most people really didn't look any further than the exterior. I found that people made all kinds of assumptions about who I was, based on what they saw. Their analysis was usually wrong. Of course I was struggling myself, trying to figure out who I was, now that my life had been turned upside down — now that everything had changed.

After my physical transformation, my ex-husband once cruelly remarked that if I had looked this good years earlier, maybe we wouldn't have divorced. I was crushed! I told him about my emptiness, my brokenness. I had once been a happy, healthy, strong, and confident woman. He had me back then. He had all of me, my spirit and my soul. That part of me was gone now. In its place was a shell — a beautiful shell, but a shell nonetheless. And he would rather have that?

Many women transform their outward appearance with cosmetic surgery today, only to find that inside, they, too, are empty. It's so important to remember that the restoration of your spirit and soul is far more critical to who you are. A beautiful exterior along with a beautiful interior is always best! Eventually, with counseling, I found that balance.

Dorothy's hair was arranged in beautiful ringlets. The Scarecrow was re-stuffed with fresh straw. The Tin Man was polished to perfection, and the Lion's mane was combed so that it crowned his face handsomely. I, too, enjoyed the beauty treatments I found in the Emerald City.

Chapter 15 | THE WIZARD OF OZ

At Glinda's suggestion, Dorothy and her friends traveled a long way to see the illustrious Wizard of Oz. Dorothy had high hopes that this Wizard might be able to assist her in getting back to Kansas. I, too, was searching for guidance. I wanted to get back to a normal, happy life. Unlike Dorothy, I didn't need a true wizard or magician. I needed a competent and accomplished professional counselor.

I had a strategy all mapped out. If I could find a good counselor, I would go first and allow the counselor to help me with my immediate crises, so that I could keep myself together. I would also use the opportunity to really examine this kind of therapeutic treatment and determine whether or not it would be good for my children, as well. I didn't take lightly the idea of any individual, trained or not, zoning into the depths of my children's minds. If all was aboveboard and went well, I would bring my girls in for counseling, too. I knew Jordan and Grace were struggling with the after-effects of the divorce, but I didn't want to expose them to anything that might be even more harmful. I did hope my Wizard of Oz would be able to help!

The girls and I agreed that our therapist needed to be a woman. We all seemed to feel most comfortable with that. Of course, the girls' counseling sessions would be private, meaning that I wouldn't be invited in. With that in mind, it was important to me that I find a Christian counselor, someone who shared the beliefs at the very foundation of our lives, as opposed to someone who might have very different values and — consciously or unconsciously — undermine the girls' faith. They had already experienced a great loss, I didn't want their faith challenged as well.

I took this counseling endeavor very seriously. I wanted to do my best to see that our experience was a positive and beneficial one. I searched high and low, and made many phone calls. Finally, thanks to the referral of a friend, I ended up at the Samaritan Counseling Services of the Gulf Coast.

OF COURSE, WHAT I STRATEGIZED IN MIND MY AND WHAT ACTUALLY HAPPENED WERE TWO VERY DIFFERENT THINGS.

Dorothy and her companions each had a specific need. For one it was a brain, for another a heart, for another courage. Dorothy, herself, needed to find a way home. My daughters and I also had very specific, yet different needs.

The divorce had affected each of our lives in very different ways. I figured we needed someone who could take each of us individually, and prescribe a unique plan for healing and recovery. Of course, what I strategized in mind my and what actually happened were two very different things.

Dorothy and her friends met the Wizard of Oz on three different occasions. At the first meeting, they would only see the robotic, mechanical façade that portrayed the Wizard as one who was mighty and to be feared. He would assign them the great challenge of bringing back to him the broomstick of the Wicked Witch of the West.

Initially, my goal was to get some good advice—some practical instruction—on what steps to take to move forward with my life. And that's what I got. Once I was moving forward, I introduced my youngest daughter, Grace, to this wise counselor. Grace was somewhat reserved at first, but agreed that she would like to attend more sessions. She was given several small assignments that seemed to help her considerably. Grace and the counselor continued to meet for several months, until Grace felt that things were better.

As Grace completed her therapy, I returned to the counselor myself. My health insurance covered these sessions with an out-of-pocket co-pay, but we still couldn't afford to all attend counseling at the same time. Once again, I found the therapy helpful, and continued twice a month for several months.

Unfortunately, just as we began to make real progress, my Wizard informed me that she was retiring and that another would be taking her place. I was disappointed and disheartened. It had taken a long time for me to open up and build a trusting relationship with the first Wizard. (I had always been a private person and sharing my true feelings was very difficult for me.) Now I would have to start over again.

I agreed to meet my counselor's replacement, and although she seemed very nice, I decided to take a little time off from therapy. I didn't know it yet, but one day this new Wizard would become an amazing confidant and advocate for me. She would help me find exactly what I was looking for! She would guide me in my journey of self-discovery, healing, and restoration, until I made my way home. That venture would take over four years.

In the meantime, my oldest daughter, Jordan, returned home from school to take a much-needed break. Jordan had left for college just after I had announced that I had filed for divorce. College is challenging enough without adding that on top of it. When she arrived, she joined the party scene with what seemed like every other student. I'm sure it offered her an easy escape from the concerns she had of her parent's breakup. Now, two and a half years had flown by, and she still had not received counseling for the damages brought on by the divorce. A semester off provided the time needed for some good counsel.

Jordan is a sweet young woman. She could never understand why whenever she did something wrong, somehow she'd always get caught. She couldn't get away with anything! I personally attribute it to the "kiss of God" upon her forehead. She's just destined for a different path. As her mother, I always viewed her "getting caught" as a blessing in disguise and an answer to my prayers. It always opened up wonderful doors of communication between us, giving me the opportunity to discuss with her life's issues and the choices it presented. It seemed that in her humbled condition she was a good listener, and God always gave me wisdom to share with her.

In this case, it was obvious that Jordan needed a time out to regroup. By the time she arrived home, we had several conversations about the college environment and its challenges. She had already confessed her disappointment with herself for getting caught up in the party scene. She'd learned her lesson and she was determined to change. I, on the other hand, was convinced there was something more to her coming home. There had to be. An honor student taking a break in the middle of the college experience? Something didn't quite make sense.

"It will all work out," I told her. "God must have a reason for you being here at this time. Let's just make the best of it, and see how it all works out."

Well, God did have a reason. A very good reason.

While she was still in school, Jordan had worked extremely hard to get her lifeguard credentials. The lifeguard testing was very challenging for her, yet she was determined to do it, and she went above and beyond in her training to qualify for the job. I remember her almost in tears, telling me how difficult some of the swim tests were for her. At the time, I wondered why it was such a big deal to her to pursue this particular job. But I was proud to see her show such diligence and determination in this challenge. In the process, Jordan was thoroughly trained in CPR. As it turned out, she would use this skill to save her brother's life.

One morning, we would wake up to find her brother, Joe, nearly dead of a drug overdose. God would use Jordan to keep her brother breathing, until the paramedics arrived. There were no awards given that day. There was no spotlight shining upon her. There was just the truth that somehow, in her humbled status of taking a semester off from school to pull it together and get back on track, God made her a hero. Had Jordan been away at college, and not at home that morning, it's highly unlikely that her brother would have survived.

"And we know that all things work together for good to those who love God." (Romans 8:28a, NKJV)

During her time at home, Jordan attended a few counseling sessions and eventually returned to her college campus feeling better. It wasn't until a year after she had graduated, gotten a job out of state, and then returned home to attend grad school that I noticed she still had a long way to go. I had made substantial progress in my journey of healing, but she couldn't even talk about the divorce without tearing up and getting upset. It was then she returned to the counseling center and found a new Wizard to help her complete her personal healing process.

Dorothy and her friends returned a second time to see the Wizard. They were in great spirits, having accomplished the practically impossible assignment of returning to Oz with the broomstick of the Wicked Witch. Unfortunately, that's when they discovered that the Great Wizard was nothing but a fraud. Beneath all the bells, whistles, and plumes of smoke, behind the curtain was a silly little man who was powerless to help them. When I think of this scene, and how it fits in with my story, I am reminded of how disappointed Baum's characters were when it dawned on them that their quest might be hopeless. They might never get their needs met.

From the start, I found that just about everyone I knew seemed to have an opinion about what I should be doing to get through my divorce. As kind-hearted as they were, as well-intended as all the advice was, it wasn't professional counseling. It didn't fit my specific needs and address my particular circumstances. By this time, the one thing I did know, and wasn't afraid to admit to myself, was that I needed the help of a professional. I returned to the counseling center to once again meet with the new Wizard who had been assigned to me.

I have to tell you, counseling was not easy. In fact, it was hard work. I faithfully attended sessions every other week for several years. I did learn to trust this new Wizard. Over time, she proved to me that she was very kind, a good listener, confidential, spiritual, and filled with wisdom, which she offered when it was needed. She helped me to talk about my feelings and what I was experiencing. We talked about my brokenness. We talked about lost dreams. We talked about rejection. We talked about my children. We talked about how to deal with life day to day. We talked about medication. We talked about dating. We talked about love. We talked about my fears. I guess we talked about everything.

I knew that I was in the right place for healing. I also knew that in order to get the most out of it, I needed to be honest and straightforward about what I was thinking. Very often the Wizard would suggest I consider a different perspective in my thinking. Sometimes I saw things from the perspective of my brokenness, instead of seeing them as they were. She helped me to understand the powerful effect of the green glasses, and how they could taint the truth.

The Wizard would also challenge me to consider things, pray about things, and to talk about what was deep within me. She helped me to get things out in the open, instead of stuffing them away. It sounds so easy, but most of the sessions were filled with an outpouring of tears. Progress for me seemed slow. Although I left each session feeling better than when I arrived, it was always an emotional challenge to get myself there each time. The weeks went by, followed by months. Months turned into seasons, and seasons into years. One of my greatest struggles was my attempt at being one hundred percent transparent with her. That took a long time, but ultimately I accomplished that. I know that if I hadn't, my healing would have been significantly hindered and delayed. Instead, I moved forward to completeness.

The Wizard of Oz reached into his bag and pulled out special gifts for Dorothy's friends… a diploma, a clock in the shape of a heart, and a badge signifying courage. It was obvious that in all of their adventures together, the Scarecrow, the Tin Man, and the Lion had in fact demonstrated the very characteristics they were hoping to find: wisdom, love, and fearless courage.

With any difficult journey, there are always invaluable gifts to be found along the way. With all the difficulties I encountered, I found I pocketed a wealth of wisdom with which to face the future and whatever it may hold for me. I broke through the rejection and pain, and found that my heart had been restored. Somehow, I learned to trust again. I also found that in facing my fears, I developed the roar of a courageous lion.

When I stand back and look at all the gifts I walked away with, there is one I could never have expected. Somehow, I fell in love with my womanhood. I had never thought much about femininity before. I was never one that had many girlfriends. I was always more interested in what the men were doing. I was intrigued by what they were thinking. I found myself competing with them to do the things that they did just as well, if not better. Most of the people I got along best with were male. I never seemed to take notice much of other women.

Now it was different. I was really proud of myself. I had made it! God knows there were many times I didn't think I would, but I did. I made it! There was no husband by my side… it was just me and God, and the friends God brought my way. When I got back to Kansas, I found I had a victorious story to tell. I also noticed there were other women all around me who had amazing stories, too! I discovered passion burning within me to speak out and give other women hope and encouragement in their journeys. I also wanted to spotlight the amazing things that the women around me were doing in life and in business. I established *Because Women LLC* to do just that.

I DISCOVERED PASSION BURNING WITHIN ME TO SPEAK OUT AND GIVE OTHER WOMEN HOPE AND ENCOURAGEMENT IN THEIR JOURNEYS.

Dorothy and her friends met one final time with the Wizard. They gathered around to say their goodbyes, as Dorothy prepared to leave for Kansas in the Wizard's big hot air balloon. When Toto jumped from Dorothy's arms, she leapt out of the balloon to retrieve him. The Wizard and the balloon took off without her.

A year before my return from Oz, the Wizard challenged me to face some of my most difficult fears. I retreated and conveniently decided to take a sabbatical from counseling. Over and over, however, I continued to ponder her advice. It seemed impossible to make some of the changes that she asked me to consider. I prayed and asked God to help me. (Perhaps she was praying, too?) These changes seemed beyond my ability. That was just about the time that I had that spiritual encounter with God in my car — the one that led me to ask my psychiatrist to take me off my medication. Before I knew it, nine or ten months had flown by without a single counseling session. And I was fine. God certainly kept His word — my life was becoming drastically different. It was changing for the better.

Shortly afterwards, I found myself home, a long way from Oz. I did return to see the Wizard to tie up some loose ends. Dorothy's Wizard may have abandoned her in Oz, but my Wizard had seen to it that I not only got home safely, but that I managed my way through the difficult, but victorious transition. Our final sessions were tear-free. It was great to have some good news to bring her for a change. Seeing my smile, I'm sure must have blessed her. Even to this day, she continues to be a trusted friend and confidant. I am very thankful for all she did for me. She truly guided me through my journey of self-discovery, healing and restoration.

Chapter 16 | THE DARK FOREST

Dorothy and her friends have been commissioned by the Great Wizard to retrieve the broomstick of the Wicked Witch of the West. They have entered the Dark Forest, which they must pass through in order to get to the Witch's castle. Their surroundings are strange and scary. Owls peer down from the tree branches, their eyes glowing in the dark. A signpost warns, "I'd turn back if I were you."

The Lion would be most happy to do just that, as he shuts his eyes tight, grasps hold of his tail, and repeats to himself over and over again: "I do believe in spooks! I do believe in spooks!"

We all come to places in life, where we'd like to turn around and run the other way. These are dark, difficult, and dangerous places—and they can't always be avoided. People often ask me, "What was the most difficult part of your journey?"

The answer is easy. It was my trip through the Dark Forest. That's where I almost lost my precious son to a drug overdose.

THIS WAS THE CRY THAT PENETRATES THE DEPTHS OF A MOTHER'S HEART. IT'S A CRY THAT'S DIFFERENT FROM ALL THE REST — A CRY FOR HELP.

That Sunday morning, I woke up to the shout of my youngest daughter. My kids have shouted for me many times. This was the cry that penetrates the depths of a mother's heart. It's a cry that's different from all the rest—a cry for help. It's not the words, but the intense tone that sends you into emergency mode immediately.

"Mom, come quick! Joe's not breathing!"

I leapt out of bed and crossed to the other side of the house in the blink of an eye. There was my son, lying back on his bed. His face was a grayish-purple, and swollen. He didn't seem to be breathing, though somehow he was making an awful snorting sound. As best as I can remember, I tried to wake him, shaking him, shouting his name, slapping his face to get some sort of response. Nothing.

"Grace, call 911. Then call your father and tell him to get over here! Jordan, get in here and help me!"

I continued to try waking my son. In my sternest voice, I called to him, "Don't you give up on me, Joey! Don't you give up!"

Within seconds, the 911 operator was on the phone, giving us instruction to move Joe onto the floor and lay him flat on his back. Jordan, being a lifeguard at college, was more equipped to take charge, so we switched places, and she took the lead. She began CPR, while I stayed on the phone and relayed information back and forth between her and the emergency operator. I counted out loud as she worked on bringing her brother back to us.

Meanwhile, my youngest daughter, Grace, went into her bedroom, closed the door, dropped to her knees, and began pleading for her brother's survival. "Not now, Lord! Please don't take him from us!" she interceded.

Jordan and I did our best to stay focused on the instructions we were being given. We couldn't allow our emotions to take over. There just wasn't time. Joe wasn't responding to Jordan's efforts, and I know it was a struggle for her, but she stayed in control. At that moment, I couldn't verbalize any kind of prayer. The name "Jesus" simply rested on my tongue and filled my heart. My God would know how to interpret that, I had no doubt.

The next thing I knew, the paramedics were arriving. They quickly lifted Joe onto a stretcher and moved him outside to work on him in the ambulance. I ran to my bedroom to throw on some clothes, knowing the next step would be to follow the ambulance to the hospital. As I was putting on my sneakers, a police officer entered my home.

"Your son is not breathing," he announced. "Do you know if he's been taking drugs?"

I told the truth. I knew Joe had been smoking pot and that he might possibly have experimented with other drugs, but I didn't know any details.

"I need to look in his room to see if we can find what he might have taken. It could help the rescue workers save your son."

Under other circumstances, I would have had him wait until my ex-husband arrived. Dave was a former police officer, and understood the legal procedures and ramifications. But you don't hesitate when your baby is dying. I immediately agreed.

Just then, Dave arrived and we briefed him on what was happening. He knew it was not a good sign that the ambulance was still outside our door, instead of on its way to the hospital. They were still trying to get Joe's breathing stabilized. Dave pulled the girls and I together in the kitchen. We held hands, as he led us in prayer for our Joe's recovery. The next thing I knew, we were en route to the hospital.

I just whispered over and over again, "Please save my son, Lord. Help, Jesus, Help!"

When we arrived, the hospital staff told us that only one parent could go into the actual emergency room. I didn't wait to ask which one. All I knew was that I was going in. I needed to see my boy. Dave would have to help the girls and figure out a way to get in there, himself.

It was a horrific site—Joe lying on that hospital bed with all those tubes sticking out of him, doctors and nurses hovering all around. I stood at the bottom of the bed, praying in the Spirit and whispering the name of Jesus to myself, over and over again. It seemed an eternity as I watched the doctors attempt to revive him.

Once they got Joe breathing, the goal was to get him to open his eyes. The doctors asked me to call his name over and over again, hoping that the familiarity of my voice would get his attention.

"Joe, it's Mom," I called. "Open your eyes Joe!"

The doctors saw a few movements that led them to believe that he could hear me. They urged me to keep trying. Eventually Joe opened his eyes. That was a huge relief, but it only lasted for a moment.

Next, they wanted to get him talking. If he couldn't talk, it meant there was brain damage. By that time, Dave was in the room with me. I remember him calling out to Joe. It was a deep, masculine-sounding voice, so very different from my own. We pleaded with Joe to talk to us, and we waited on edge for his response.

It seemed like forever, but after a few minutes, Joe did begin to talk to us. It could not have happened soon enough! We were so relieved.

I had completely forgotten that the girls were in the waiting room all this time, crying and praying for their brother, anxiously waiting for a report. I later learned that in the midst of her tears, Grace had heard God speak to her.

"Joe's going to be alright. Don't you remember all the things I've shown you about Joe? This is just a passage that he has to take, in order for him to get where he needs to be. This is not the end. Joe's going to be alright."

Grace immediately wiped away her tears, and comforted her sister with what she had heard. A peace came over her. She knew that this was not the end.

With the worst moments behind us, we regrouped as a family, while Joe was being moved to the Intensive Care Unit. There were phone calls to be made, as we moved to the waiting room on another floor. Honestly, I have no memory of making any of these calls, but I must have, because a number of people soon arrived to offer their love and support. The Scarecrow stopped by to make sure all was okay. The Lion came and never left. A friend of Dave's brought food for those of us in the waiting room. I wouldn't necessarily have called my extended family, but my sister and a good friend were visiting Florida at the time, and the Lion convinced me that it was important to bring them in on this. They immediately rushed to my side. I didn't want to worry my mother, but again, the Lion encouraged me to tell her what had happened, and I later followed his advice.

The girls went in to see Joe, to talk with him and pray with him. He was tired and groggy and totally oblivious to what had happened. We were going through the most difficult (potentially devastating) experience of our entire lives, but he slept through it all. He didn't get it. It wasn't until his father showed him a picture of himself in the ER, taken with a cell phone, that he realized what had transpired. Even then, he couldn't really take it all in. He was too exhausted and uncomfortable. Far from being grateful or relieved to be alive, he was downright grumpy and miserable.

As I roamed the hospital corridors, worn out and somewhat discouraged, two wonderful Christian people stepped out of the elevator. Mr. and Mrs. Ditchfield had come to visit their oldest daughter in the hospital, while she recovered from knee surgery. We bumped into each other unexpectedly in the hallway. We had met briefly on a couple of occasions, but I didn't know them very well. Their other daughter was a friend of mine. I do know this—at that moment, I desperately needed the reassurance that God was with me, and looking back now, if I could have chosen one person in Sarasota who reflected that image of God, it was Mr. Ditchfield. I remember the incredible strength and love I felt as Stephen reached out his arms and huddled his wife and I into a circle and prayed for my son. They were like angels sent from God to give me hope.

IT NEVER CEASES TO AMAZE ME HOW GOD BRINGS US EXACTLY WHAT WE NEED, WHEN WE NEED IT.

It never ceases to amaze me how God brings us exactly what we need, when we need it.

"My God will meet all your needs..." (Philippians 4:19a)

Several days went by, and Joe was moved to another part of the hospital. Although he was out of the woods now, there were still some things that needed to be addressed—he needed to be confronted about the behaviors that had gotten him into this mess. I didn't know what I was in for, as I headed to my son's room that night to meet with him, his dad and his sisters. The conversation certainly couldn't have been too unexpected for Joe. I had been pondering for days on how we would deal with this whole drug issue, now that the worst was behind us. I wanted Joe to face his addiction and overcome it. I asked him to go into a Christian drug program called Teen Challenge.

As a family, we were all familiar with the Teen Challenge program. Good friends of ours had been overseers of a Teen Challenge program for years. A number of the churches we had attended financially supported the Teen Challenge ministry, and we had heard many times the personal testimonies of individuals who had been delivered from addiction to drugs due to the success of the program. A faith-based program like Teen Challenge seemed the natural road to take. I had already called and found a local program about an hour away. It was affordable.

I was completely taken back when Joe refused to discuss it. He had no intention of going into any program. He didn't even like the idea of seeing a counselor. He was adamant about it. Since he was refusing to get treatment, I told him that he couldn't come home. The girls and I had been pushed to our limit, emotionally. We needed a break. He'd have to move in with his dad.

I was trying to exercise tough love. I thought he would give in and go to the program, but that's not how he responded. Suddenly, I felt an avalanche of hopelessness rushing down on me.

"Why won't you do what I ask?" I cried. "Why won't you just go in this program? I have never steered you wrong. I have never lied to you. I have never done anything but love you and help you. Why won't you just trust me and do what I'm telling you to do?"

It only seemed to anger him. Later I learned how hurt and rejected he felt when I announced that he couldn't come home. As he stared at me in silence and stubbornly held his ground, I turned to walk out the door and collapsed on the floor. Curled up into a fetal position, I wept, as every bit of hope drained from my body. My girls desperately tried to get me up off the floor. Joe seemed unmoved. I felt that instead of seeing the depth of my love for him and the grief and pain I experienced on his behalf, Joe saw only a weak, emotional mess of a mother. I got to my feet again, and walked out the room, heading down the corridor to the area where the Lion was patiently waiting. He took my hand and walked me out to the parking lot. I felt numb. I was withdrawn. The Lion drove me home, trying his best to encourage me. I know my lack of response worried him.

Joe wasn't coming home. I didn't like this tough love. I wanted to blame all the people who had told me to take this stand, but I trusted their wisdom—I knew this approach was right. It was hard, but necessary. I just wished Joe had agreed to get help. It would have been a much easier road, for him and for the rest of us.

Weeks went by. I saw Joe almost everyday, but it wasn't the same as having him home. My heart ached for him. He was with his dad, and I realized that Dave might be better for him than I was right now. Maybe he needed a strong, male authority figure in his life at this time. The girls and I tried to move on with our lives, taking one day at a time.

Joe's dad and I continued to have many conversations with him about getting his life back on the right track. Joe's uncle, who had been our pastor for years, came and spent time with Joe, counseling him and helping him set some goals. The family support was amazing, but ultimately Joe was the one who had to take responsibility for his life. It seemed an awful lot for a nineteen year old boy to handle. In our conversations, I often felt awkward, like I was walking on eggshells. I wanted to be firm, but not harsh. I didn't want to turn him away from me, from his family, from God. If he turned away from everyone who loved him, he would turn toward the only other thing he knew at that time: his friends and drugs. There was one thing I was very grateful for: there were many, many people constantly lifting him up in prayer. Family, friends, friends of friends, church members past and present, near and far—everybody knew what had happened. They all loved Joe and began to pray for him. That was a very good thing!

For me, the experience led to a bit of a setback. Although I was already in counseling and on medication, nearly losing my son had brought great fear into my life. Fear can be gripping. It can put a stranglehold on you, and take your breath away. It can paralyze you. But God is bigger than our fears.

The Bible says, "For God has not given us a spirit of fear, but of power, and of love, and of a sound mind." (2 Timothy 1:7 NKJV)

He delivered me from my fear, late one evening, in my son's bedroom.

I had not been able to go into Joe's room for some time. Just looking at it brought back visions of all that had happened that dreadful morning, along with the intense emotions I had experienced. This evening however, I went inside and stayed awhile. I looked around. I prayed.

"Even in his absence, his clothes still found their way to the floor," I chuckled softly. As I started to pick them up, I found myself holding the clothes up to my nose, breathing in deeply. My heart was filled with the wonderful, loving thoughts a mother holds for her son, as I took in his scent. It was a wonderful smell. Suddenly I fell to my knees, and the tears began to flow, as the presence of God filled the room. I poured out my heart to God, and when I couldn't cry anymore, I heard His voice.

"Gail, let go." (There was a pause.) "It's okay. When you let go of Joe, you'll find that My arms are right under yours.

Let me take it from here. I'll take care of Joe… That's it. I've got him now."

Peace filled my heart as I knelt on that floor. I stood up, knowing that the responsibility for Joe had changed hands. The presence of God left the room, and so did I. I emerged still a mother, but a mother delivered from fear. My hope was restored. From that point on, I walked forward with my head high, knowing that God was in control—not just of my life, but of Joe's.

Eventually Joe would move back home. God would take Joe down a different path than the one I would have chosen for him. But I discovered that different paths can lead to the same place. I am happy to say that as I write this now, Joe's life has changed miraculously for the better. It's still a work in progress, though one day he'll be telling the details of this testimony—his testimony—to many. And God will get the glory!

I DISCOVERED THAT DIFFERENT PATHS CAN LEAD TO THE SAME PLACE.

Late one evening, a few months after Joe's trip to the emergency room, there was a knock at my door. A police officer was looking for Joe; he had a warrant for his arrest. Apparently, the day Joe was taken by ambulance to the hospital, the police officer had found some pills in his bedroom. They were here now to arrest him for drug possession. Joe wasn't staying with me at the time, so the police officer asked me to inform him of the warrant the next time I saw him. I did see Joe a few days later, and convinced him to turn himself in.

That Sunday was Mother's Day. Joe and I met for breakfast, then went to the police station together. I had called a bail bondsman, who met us there, and we went through the required procedures. It didn't seem to have a major impact on Joe, but it was a new and humbling experience for me.

Joe was free to go until his court appearance, scheduled for a date several months away. In the meantime, in return for the bond I paid, Joe went with me to see a lawyer. The lawyer got Joe into a program called Drug Court that promised to wipe out the federal charges against him, as long as he completed the treatment. Joe agreed.

Although Joe still hung out with many of his same friends, he took responsibility for fulfilling the requirements of the program. Every morning he called in to see if he had to submit that day to a mandatory drug test. Usually there were two or three drug tests a week. If he didn't test clean, he would have to appear before a judge and be sentenced either to community service or to spend a night or two in jail. There was always a risk that he could get thrown out of the program. He had to go to a counseling session every week, and attend several AA (Alcoholics Anonymous) or NA (Narcotics Anonymous) meetings. With little to no help from me, he kept his commitments and fulfilled the requirements of the program.

A few months later, Joe was pulled in by the police. His fingerprints had been found on a vehicle from which some electronic equipment had been stolen. Although the charge was later dropped, that action set off a series of actions that revoked his bail, and he ended up in the local county jail for several weeks. How I could end up with a son in jail was beyond my understanding. I had made a diligent effort to raise my kids with the kind of discipline and values that would keep them out of this kind of trouble. We were not only a Christian family, but a family in full-time Christian ministry for years. We took our faith seriously! I had stayed home instead of working to give my children a good foundation in life. I had even home-schooled them, putting off public school for several years, in an attempt to keep them from unhealthy influences while they were still young. So how, after all that effort, did Joe wind up in jail?

I'm still not really sure what the answer is. I don't think it's a simple one; I think it's a combination of many factors. I'm sure the divorce played a role. Perhaps the turmoil of adolescence had something to do with it. Joe's poor choices certainly steered things in the wrong direction. Years later, I remembered that just prior to Joe's experimentation with drugs, he had been prescribed a medication for acne that had serious potential side effects, including depression. Could the medication have pushed him over the edge and into drugs? I'm not sure.

But this I do know: God was faithful.

Looking back, it was a very scary time for me. I had no idea what to do, where to go, or who to talk to—but I figured it out. It was over a week before we were allowed to visit Joe in jail. In that time, he had enrolled himself in the "God Pod" group. He met some wonderful ministers who regularly visited prisons to conduct services for the inmates. In one sense, it was actually a relief to know where Joe was every night. I wrote him letters every day. Those letters contained some of the most serious, straight-forward words I had ever exchanged with him, and they were packed with lots of motherly love. I knew God was working on Joe, and I was okay.

NOW I HAD TO WONDER: HOW MANY MOTHERS THOUGHT THEIR KIDS WOULD BE MUCH BETTER OFF IF THEY DIDN'T HANG AROUND WITH MY SON?

Through all of this, an amazing insight hit me. I used to think that if Joe didn't hang around with those friends of his, his life would be so much better. Joe was a good kid. Really, he was. People in the community, like teachers and doctors and dental assistants would often come up to me and say, "I just wanted to meet Joe Sullivan's mom! He is the nicest young man—so personable!" When the drugs got a hold of him, though, they changed him. He wasn't the same person anymore. The drugs took control. Now I had to wonder: How many mothers thought their kids would be much better off if they didn't hang around with my son? In reality, Joe and his friends were all good kids, but when the drugs got hold of them, they all changed. It's a humbling experience, when you realize that you can't point the finger at anyone else.

Joe was eventually released from jail, and all of the charges against him were dropped. He completed the Drug Court program successfully. He got a job and continued with his college studies. I'm very proud of Joe. He's worked very hard to get off—and stay off—the prescription drugs that nearly took his life. God has been right there by his side, every step of the way. Joe has also been greatly blessed by the support of his family, church, and friends.

Looking back, I don't regret the steps I took to raise my children with a good, solid, Christian foundation. The sacrifices I made as a young mother were an important investment in my children's lives. When Joe was in the hospital, and later when he was in jail, it was difficult to see the profit of that investment. Now, however, several years later, I can see the immense value of it in each of my children's lives. It certainly has paid off.

This Dark Forest experience of mine (and of Joe's) lasted a couple of years. I have learned not to let a short detour determine how I evaluate the progress of a journey that can take a lifetime. Though I would never have chosen to travel through this Dark Forest, it was in this place that my perspective on many things changed for the better. I emerged with some invaluable treasures. I discovered empathy for others going through such difficult experiences. I came away with a greater understanding of God's faithfulness. I developed a passion to see young people delivered from their bondage to drugs. And I gained a greater respect, love and appreciation for my son.

I ALSO CONTINUE TO THIS DAY, TO BELIEVE BY FAITH, THAT GOD IS IN CONTROL... EVEN OF THOSE THINGS THAT APPEAR SO OUT OF CONTROL.

I also continue to this day, to believe by faith, that God is in control… even of those things that appear so out of control. My God is amazing! He has a way of miraculously bringing it all together in the end for his glory! Sometimes that happens on the spot, and other times, I have to wait to see the Grande Finale. Regardless, my applause goes to Him!

Chapter 17 | THE FLYING MONKEYS

Dorothy and her friends hadn't been in the Dark Forest for long, when they were attacked by those infamous flying monkeys. In all my life, I have never met anyone who watched the movie as a child, and wasn't absolutely terrified of those dastardly creatures. The nasty little beasts appeared to have been under a spell of some kind, because apparently, they were at the mercy of the Wicked Witch, always on call and awaiting her orders.

In Baum's book, the Witch saw Dorothy and her friends heading in her direction, through the forest. Different from the movie, this witch had one single eye, similar to that of a telescope, and could see anything from afar. When her other minions failed to kill Dorothy and her friends, the Witch resorted to the flying monkeys. She instructed this diabolical army of spell struck primates to destroy all of the travelers, except one. They were to bring the Lion back to her castle, where she would harness him and use him like a work horse. All she wanted from Dorothy was the shoes!

The monkeys took to the air with their mission in mind. They swooped down, scooped up the Tin Man and carried him off to a rocky place. Dropping him from a great height, he was left alone, dented and broken by the sharp rocks below. The Scarecrow's clothes were ripped to pieces and all the stuffing was pulled out of his body, until he was a shapeless, unrecognizable mess. The Lion was tied up in ropes and brought to the Witch, who caged him in a gated yard behind her castle.

At this point in the story, an important truth is revealed. When the treacherous gang of monkeys swooped down to grab Dorothy and Toto, the leader took note of Glinda's kiss still resting on Dorothy's forehead, and motioned to the others not to harm her. They understood that the power of Glinda's goodness far surpassed the evil power of the Wicked Witch of the West. They dared not disrespect it! All they could do to appease the Witch was to drop Dorothy and her dog on her doorstep.

I find a fascinating parallel here. So many Christians don't realize the power of God's protection over them via the blood of Jesus. I remember singing that old-time hymn in church, "There is power, power, wonder-working power, in the blood of the Lamb!"

This power was foreshadowed in Scripture by the Passover. During the Plagues, when the Jewish people were still held captive as slaves in Egypt, Moses instructed them to mark their doorposts with the blood of a lamb, so that the Angel of Death would see it and pass over them, leaving their first-born children unharmed, while those of the Egyptians died. With Jesus' sacrificial death on the cross, all who believe in Him are (in a spiritual sense) marked with His blood—set apart as His.

I BELIEVE THIS IS TRUE IN MY OWN LIFE... THAT THERE IS AN INVISIBLE "KISS" OF GOD ON MY FOREHEAD THAT CLEARLY SIGNIFIES THAT I AM IN DIVINE PARTNERSHIP WITH GOD, AND WARNS THE ENEMY OF MY SOUL: "THIS ONE IS MINE!"

I believe this is true in my own life… that there is an invisible "kiss" of God on my forehead that clearly signifies that I am in divine partnership with God, and warns the enemy of my soul: "THIS ONE IS MINE!"

When evil comes my way, it recognizes this seal of the Spirit, and its power to harm me is severely limited. The Apostle Paul wrote that nothing can snatch the believer from the hand of God.

> "For I am convinced that neither death nor life, neither angels nor demons, neither the present nor the future, nor any powers, neither height nor depth, nor anything else in all creation will be able to separate us from the love of God that is in Christ Jesus our Lord." (Romans 3:38-40)

Chapter 18 | THE WICKED WITCH OF THE WEST

Many children today still fear the green-faced Wicked Witch of the West, thanks to Margaret Hamilton's outstanding portrayal in the movie version of *The Wizard of Oz*. Who can forget that close-up shot, in which she threatens Dorothy, "I'll get you my little pretty, and your little dog, too!"

Perhaps we should have guessed that the Witch wasn't quite as powerful as she seemed, when she cowered before Glinda and the warning that she should watch out, lest a house fall on her, too.

Late in their journey, Dorothy and Toto were lifted into the air by the flying monkeys and delivered at the feet of the Wicked Witch. Baum's book reveals a second important truth. Not only did the Witch immediately notice the kiss on Dorothy's forehead, she trembled at the sight of the shoes on Dorothy's feet. She was petrified, knowing just how powerful they made Dorothy—until she realized that Dorothy didn't get it. Even though Dorothy had been told that the shoes were enchanted, and that they would protect her and that she should always keep them on her feet, she really didn't understand how powerful they were, or how they worked. The Witch, in turn, deceived Dorothy into becoming her servant, with the threat that if she failed to obey the Witch's commands, she would end up like the Tin Man and the Scarecrow. The Witch didn't even have to exercise any black magic. She just talked a lot of smack, and Dorothy succumbed.

It's the same for so many of us who are Christians. We can recite dozens of Scriptures about the power of God in the believer's life, yet so often instead of responding to challenges with courage and confidence, we retreat in fear. We're worse than Dorothy, in that we know the truth. It's all around us. We can read it in the Bible, listen to it in our churches, on television or on the radio. It's on greeting cards and coffee mugs and bumper stickers. But when the rubber meets the road, we don't respond in faith. If we did, we'd stand firm. We would laugh in the face of danger. We would move forward in victory time and time again.

ALTHOUGH I CAME CLOSE TO THE EDGE MANY TIMES IN MY JOURNEY, I NEVER FELL OFF.

In my case, I know that my brokenness affected my perception of things. I didn't feel like much of a warrior. I will say that I was fortunate to have been a praying woman for many, many years. Like deposits in a bank account, I had stored up strength which I drew from. But more importantly, I had the "kiss" of God upon me. Although I came close to the edge many times in my journey, I never fell off. Like Dorothy and her magical slippers, I had the Holy Spirit with me. The angels of God were all around me. Though I wasn't always aware of it, there were many times when I should have been down for the count. Somehow I always got back up. Many times I was stopped dead in my tracks, convinced I couldn't take another step. Yet I found the strength to try again. When my dreams were dashed and along with that, my sense of purpose, I found a new hope and a new vision. So often trouble came right up to my face, then turned in another direction. Yes, as I look back, I could have done more. I should have done more! The fact that I didn't *feel* like a warrior didn't mean I wasn't a warrior. But even in my defeated mindset. God brought me through.

"The steps of a good man are ordered by the Lord."
(Psalm 37:23 NKJV)

On the yellow brick road, the kiss and the shoes are key! Now that I'm back in Kansas, where I'm strong again, I try to remember that they still are, and I still have them. Each day, I have the promise that I can do all things through Christ who strengthens me. (Philippians 4:13) I stand more firmly in my recognition that "with God on my side, who can be against me? There is no reason to fear."

When the Wicked Witch tries to take Dorothy's shoes by force, she finds that she cannot. The shoes resist her power. At that point, she screams at Dorothy, "I'll never have those shoes as long as you're alive!" She continually plots to kill the girl, using any and all of her powers.

There is another amazing truth to be captured here.

"The thief (the devil) comes only to steal, and kill and destroy..." (John 10:10a)

This enemy of our soul doesn't want us to fulfill our God-given destiny. Each one of us was created for a reason. There's something God intends for us to accomplish on this earth! The devil will try everything in his power to discourage us, deceive us, or delete us. If he can take us out completely, he will. If he can get us to party our lives away in a field of poppies, that's just as good. If he can just keep us as far away from God as possible, so that we don't make a divine connection, he'll settle for that.

But God is working even harder to get the message to us that He loves us, and that He has a plan and a purpose for us. He wants so much for us to connect with Him.

"I have come that they might have life, and have it to the full." (John 10:10b)

I am a firm believer that in the darkest moments, the light shines brightest. One day, you may find yourself feeling empty, alone, or in the deepest and darkest of pits. Never underestimate the incredible power of the simplest, heartfelt prayer: "Help me God!"

I AM A FIRM BELIEVER THAT IN THE DARKEST MOMENTS, THE LIGHT SHINES BRIGHTEST.

So often, that's the turning point. That is where things start to change. In that moment, when we acknowledge that we need help, when we wonder if God is really there, when we believe just enough to call on Him... Yes, that is where the earth shakes and the mountains are moved. That is where the miraculous occurs. Sometimes it's hard to believe, because it's so simple. But the amazing truth is that when you call on God, He answers.

Chapter 19 | THE CRYSTAL BALL

As Dorothy sat trapped in the Witch's castle, watching the sand flow through the hour glass, her eyes caught a glimpse of the Witch's crystal ball. As she moved in to take a closer look, there was Aunt Em calling to her, "Dorothy! Where are you?" Then Dorothy saw the face of the Wicked Witch shouting back in her nasty voice, "I'm afraid Aunty Em, I'm afraid!" followed by that shrill evil laugh. Dorothy pulled back, more fearful than ever, as the Witch's evil power overwhelmed her.

Of course the whole thing is part of the dream that is Dorothy's journey through Oz. In reality, Dorothy is fast asleep in her own bed, with Aunt Em by her side. Yet it all seems so real.

The crystal ball has significance to me because it reminds me of the tormenting deception I continually battled against in my journey to mental, emotional, and spiritual well-being.

Once I got off of all the medication I'd been taking, I could think more clearly. But I found that I was easily distracted. For some reason, any negative thought or concern that could possibly come to mind did—and it wasn't so easy to get rid of it. Just as the Witch tried to use the frightening images in the crystal ball to manipulate Dorothy into thinking a certain way, I felt the enemy was trying to use fear to manipulate my thoughts and prevent me from moving forward in my journey. I was constantly bombarded by fears of rejection, failure, and incompetence.

"Where are they all coming from?" I wondered. When I was crippled by my pain, it seemed there were no obstacles in my path. Now, however, just as I was regaining my strength and heading for true healing… BOOM! I was being hit from all sides with what seemed like blow after blow!

Frustrated, I tried to remember what I'd learned about the importance of disciplining one's thoughts and the impact that reading the Scriptures could have in what was surely some kind of spiritual warfare. I decided to take action and return to the basics. I started a schedule of daily Bible reading to counter the commotion in my mind. I started each day with a brief devotional reading. Every night I meditated on a few verses before I went to bed. I also read a great book that I highly recommend—Joyce Meyer's *Battlefield of the Mind,* and I followed her godly guidance. I regularly attended a church, where I heard good, solid Bible teaching. And I made a point of choosing to listen to positive, uplifting Christian music as I drove in my car. The results were amazing!

THIS IS NOT TO SAY THAT THE BATTLE WAS OVER IN A DAY. I HAD TO REALLY DISCIPLINE MYSELF TO FEED MY HEART, MY MIND, AND MY SPIRIT CONSISTENTLY.

This is not to say that the battle was over in a day. I had to really discipline myself to feed my heart, my mind, and my spirit consistently. It wasn't easy at first, but the daily Scripture readings were like a soothing balm calming the chaos of my mind. Slowly, the negativity drifted away, and my thoughts became more reflective of my heart's desire. In one sense, all I had to do was open the Book and read. The Holy Spirit did the rest. He brought to light the truths in God's Word that shut down the lies of the enemy. The Bible reminded me of my strength in God, of the promise of what I was destined for, and the victory that lay ahead.

On my journey, I've learned that the enemy of our soul will throw all the lies he can our way, in an attempt to derail us and defeat us. Yet the Holy Spirit will bring the truths of God to light, exposing every deception. So often God just wants us to take one step… Then He takes two, on our behalf. Truly the battle is the Lord's!

Chapter 20 | CLICK, CLICK, CLICK

When the Wizard flies off in his balloon, leaving Dorothy and Toto behind, Dorothy feels heartbroken and hopeless. After all the amazing things that had happened in her journey through Oz, her greatest desire was still to return home to Kansas. Unexpectedly, in the last hour, Glinda the Good appears once more from the sky. Dorothy's hope is restored when Glinda assures her that all will be well. Lo and behold, Dorothy learns that her ruby slippers have had the power to take her home, all along. Glinda tells Dorothy to click the heels of the magical shoes together three times, and repeat the words: "There's no place like home. There's no place like home." In seconds, Dorothy is back in Kansas. Her journey is over.

For me, however, those three clicks were months apart, and the transition from Oz to home took some time. The first click actually took place about a year before my return, shortly after the experience in the car with God and my deliverance from that over-medicated state. Click #1 was all about preparing to return home, taking all the lessons I'd learned and pulling it all together. It required some effort on my part, but as with Dorothy, most of it was about the power of the shoes.

IT REQUIRED SOME EFFORT ON MY PART, BUT AS WITH DOROTHY, MOST OF IT WAS ABOUT THE POWER OF THE SHOES.

During this time, the idea for this book seemed to drop into my lap. And with it came the hope and dream that a new ministry lay ahead for me. I held on tightly to the words God had spoken to me:

1. Don't give up!

2. In a year's time, your life will be dramatically different.

3. The visions, the gifts, the ministry... All of this awaits you, and these are only the things I've told you about. There's so much more.

I knew if ministry lay ahead, I needed to be in a church that I could call home. That was so important to me. I had been walking alone with God, more or less, since I came to Florida. It was good for a season, but I knew God had established the Church for a reason. He didn't intend for us to go through all of life alone. God gifts us with people to fellowship with in life. A church also offers much needed accountability.

As I attended my daughter Grace's church, I felt new life in the Spirit awakening within me. My first thought was that I would stay there. Unfortunately, in talking with the pastors there, God showed me that door was closed. I would have to find another church as my covering.

Several days went by. Riding in an elevator, feeling discouraged, I cried out to God. As I leaned my head back against the wall, I pleaded, "God, where am I to go? I need a home church!"

A few hours later, Grace and I were running late to a school graduation dinner. Because of our tardy arrival, we were seated at the head table with the director of the choral group and the vice principal of the school. It seemed those were the only remaining seats available. A lovely woman began a conversation with me, and out of the blue, invited me to attend her church that weekend. "It's primarily an African American church," she said, "But I think you should come."

No one had invited me to church for decades, and the day that I asked God to lead me to a new church, I got a specific invitation. I was willing to believe that this just might be the answer to my prayer.

I went to that church the very next Sunday. It was a completely new cultural experience for me, and I loved it! I already knew most of the songs. I was able to close my eyes and just worship God. Then the people around me began to vibrantly praise God in a way I hadn't seen in a long time. I just jumped right in with them, and allowed my heart to shout out to God with thanksgiving. If that weren't enough, through the pastor's message it seemed as if God was talking specifically to me. It was such a blessed time!

I continued to return to that church every Sunday. The people were so nice. For the most part, they just gave me the space and the freedom to worship God. I lifted my hands and soaked up the presence of the Lord each week. I laughed. I cried. I praised! Week after week, God continued to speak directly to me through the preaching. I couldn't believe what was happening. Although the pastor knew nothing about me or my circumstances, the teachings in his sermons seemed specifically directed to me. It had to be a God-thing!

EVERY TIME I WALKED THROUGH THE DOORS, I ENVISIONED MY HOPES AND DREAMS BECOMING REALITY.

At this point I was still living in Oz, but each Sunday was a spiritual escape for me. My heart was filled with hope, as I sensed the restoration taking place within me week after week. Health and wholeness began to inhabit my being. This church of mighty praise brought the power of healing full-force into my life! It seemed that all things were possible in this Spirit-soaked atmosphere. Every time I walked through the doors, I envisioned my hopes and dreams becoming reality. It wasn't that I was trying to convince myself that my dreams could become reality. It's that I saw in my soul the desires of my heart coming into existence. Perhaps that's what we call a vision? Regardless, I didn't experience that positive, life-changing energy anywhere else, so I just kept going back.

Nearly a year later, there was a meeting scheduled for the women of the church and I decided to attend. During that event, everyone went around in a circle and introduced themselves. The following Sunday, many of them greeted me by name. In fact, they began to call me "Sister Gail." I hadn't heard that term of endearment for over nine years. The women of the church didn't know it, but when I had been a pastor's wife, this was how many of my parishioners used to address me in love. It truly touched my heart.

The Bible teaches that God gives each of His children spiritual gifts and talents. As my spiritual health improved, the gifts God's Spirit had given me began to emerge. The minister recognized these gifts, encouraged me to use them, and told me there was a place for me in this church. I was so afraid of being rejected, but these people didn't reject me. They opened their arms to me, embraced me and all I was, and loved me! It's amazing what can happen when the Spirit of God is at work.

God had given me a home base. I officially became a member of Trinity Christian Fellowship Center. Three days later, I realized that my deliverance from Oz was complete—I had left that place for good and returned home to Normalcy. I know it was the power of the Holy Spirit, ignited by this church's praise, worship and Holy Ghost preaching, that catapulted me home!

The second click of my heels took place within weeks of the first. But just as with the first click, it took about a year to experience the full effect. As I realized that I was finally preparing to leave Oz and return home, I became acutely aware of the fact that that might mean leaving my traveling companions behind. I didn't know if I'd see them on the other side. The question came to me: "Do you really want to leave?"

THE DIFFICULTY WAS IN LETTING GO OF THE PEOPLE I HAD GROWN TO LOVE THROUGH THESE MOST DIFFICULT AND DARKEST OF TIMES.

I meditated on this for months. It was grueling. Of course I wanted to go home! This journey had been all about self-discovery, healing, and restoration. It was about getting back to normal, about finding wellness and wholeness again. But Oz has a way of getting a hold on you. I had made some good friends in Oz. There were many triumphs in Oz. I knew that on the other side, more triumphs would come through my writing. The difficulty was in letting go of the people I had grown to love through these most difficult and darkest of times.

In the movie version of *The Wizard of Oz*, Dorothy returns to find the familiar faces of her dear friends all around her. Her traveling companions had a place in her life back in Kansas, only in different roles. Would that be the case for me? I feared that my new life would sweep me off in such a different direction that I wouldn't have much in common with these friends anymore. I desperately hoped that wouldn't happen. How could I leave SK behind? I relied on his faithful friendship day after day to help me keep it all together. TW and I had become such good friends, too. Would my new life in Kansas return our friendship to what it was before—non-existent? And what about the Lion? We had grown so close. He always wondered, as did I, if our close relationship would remain intact when I left Oz—when the dynamics of our relationship and the details of our circumstances changed. It was one thing traveling together through Oz forever with him, but could I make that same commitment back in Kansas? I dragged my feet in discouragement over this for a long time.

In L. Frank Baum's book, the scene where Dorothy says goodbye to her friends is my favorite part of the story:

"Your Silver Shoes will carry you over the desert," replied Glinda. "If you had known their power you could have gone back to your Aunt Em the very first day you came to this country."

"But then I should not have had my wonderful brains!" cried the Scarecrow. "I might have passed my whole life in the farmer's cornfield."

"And I should not have had my lovely heart," said the Tin Woodman. "I might have stood and rusted in the forest till the end of the world."

"And I should have lived a coward forever," declared the Lion, "and no beast in all the forest would have had a good word to say to me."

"This is all true," said Dorothy, "and I am glad I was of use to these good friends. But now that each of them has had what he most desired, and each is happy in having a kingdom to rule besides, I think I should like to go back to Kansas."

I believe that my traveling companions and I were truly brought together for a variety of reasons. I know that they each impacted my life positively and I believe they'd say I did the same for them– That's what friends do! Now it was time for me to leave Oz. I would have to trust that the God who brought these wonderful people into my life would continue to work things out for the best in each of our lives. If He led us in different directions, I would have to accept that. My answer to His question was "Yes!" Yes, I wanted to go home. Yes, I wanted full restoration and healing. Yes, I wanted to move forward into all that God had planned for my life. It would take a huge step of faith, but at all costs, I knew I had to go on!

The third click took place on a specific date: May 20, 2009. It was on that day that I woke up with a thought at the forefront of my mind: "Today is YOUR day!" It was as clear as it could be. I was so excited! I didn't know for sure all that it meant, but I knew the date was special. I wrote it down.

Over the next couple of days, I realized that things were different inside of me. Everything seemed a little off-kilter. Only it felt good. It felt normal! Oh my gosh… I was home!!! I remember looking into a mirror, and seeing that Oz was behind me—on the other side. I wasn't there anymore! I was somewhere else. I was here. I was home. My mind was strong and healthy. My heart was new and happy. My vision was clear. Everything had been restored. It almost seemed as if it happened overnight—but no, it had been four and a half years that I had been away.

Chapter 21 | THERE'S NO PLACE LIKE HOME

As *The Wizard of Oz* comes to an end, Dorothy is back in Kansas, safe and sound in her own bed, surrounded by all of her friends and family. I always wondered what happened to Dorothy after that. Later I learned that L. Frank Baum had written many other books about Dorothy and her friends and their adventures together. So as it turns out, her story was just beginning. My story was just beginning, too.

At first, I could only focus on moving forward. To do that, I needed to absorb and apply all the things I'd learned that would keep me anchored safely here at home. I continued to attend the church that had been so instrumental in my healing through fellowship, praise, and the preaching of God's Word. I began to spend more time in personal prayer as well. It was important to stay positive and stay focused on what lay ahead. I had to consciously choose to move forward everyday. I couldn't look back. It would only delay my progress.

I HAD TO CONSCIOUSLY CHOOSE TO MOVE FORWARD EVERYDAY. I COULDN'T LOOK BACK.

There was no going back. Things had changed. The old habits that were part of the way I functioned or coped with my brokenness began slowly to fall away. I was regaining the habits of a strong, healthy woman. Skills and talents I hadn't used for ages resurfaced again. It had been so long, I was surprised I hadn't lost them in the journey!

With my new gained strength, I made great progress in the writing of my story. Constantly remembering the victory over all I had come through brought forth the vision of a company whose mission was to encourage and help other women. A greater wisdom emerged from my journey. I am passionate about making sure that this trip to Oz wasn't in vain. I hope to bring the expertise of my travels to the forefront that others might benefit.

When Dorothy returned to Kansas, she discovered the magic slippers had disappeared from her feet. But the Holy Spirit still vibrantly resides in my heart and guides my footsteps day by day. In this new place, I have grown and blossomed far more than I ever could have imagined. And I can be caught, on occasion, wearing bold red shoes that remind me of the strength and power that's within me.

I'm amazed at how things can change so much over time. Dorothy went from Kansas to Oz and back again. I have gone from a normal life to the far edge, and returned a changed woman. I wake up each day refreshed and ready for the next adventure — although, like Dorothy, I must admit:

"There's no place like home!"

Closing Remarks

The goal of this book is to bring hope to women, all over the world, who find themselves in a difficult place.

Please let us know how this book has encouraged you.
Send your emails to:
Gail@TheYellowBrickRoadBook.com

Your prayer requests are always welcome!

Additional books can be purchased online at:
www.TheYellowBrickRoadBook.com

LaVergne, TN USA
09 July 2010
188909LV00002B/9/P